MAURICE HAYES

BLACK PUDDINGS WITH SLIM
A Downpatrick Boyhood

Maurice Hayes

THE
BLACKSTAFF
PRESS

BELFAST

First published in 1996 by
The Blackstaff Press Limited
3 Galway Park, Dundonald, Belfast BT16 0AN, Northern Ireland

© Maurice Hayes, 1996
All rights reserved

Typeset by Techniset Typesetters, Newton-le-Willows, Merseyside

Printed by The Guernsey Press Company Limited

A CIP catalogue record for this book
is available from the British Library

ISBN 0-85640-590-6

for
Clodagh, Margaret,
Dara, Garrett and Rowan

... many haunting presences

Which will shadow you always, beckoning
Still, however far your country.

from 'Provincia deserta'
NORMAN DUGDALE

ONE

THERE IT WAS SITTING CORNERWISE IN THE centre of the view, a strange brick building with a clock tower, odd to find in such a place, slightly exotic. In the afternoon sunshine it looked like one of the houses in the illustrated tale of Marco Polo, a minor Venetian palace that had finally decided to give itself up to the sea and had floated up the Quoile to beach itself here at the convergence of all the roads in Downpatrick. This was the town hall.

It marked the meeting point too, as I could read from the street nameplates, of English Street, Irish Street and Scotch Street. At first I thought this puzzling and intriguing, but afterwards I decided it was symbolic of the mix that made the town and us what it was and what we were.

I clambered down out of the lofty cab of Billy Nolan's lorry to inspect this new wonder and to enter a new world. This building, which was a focus for the town, was to become a major landmark for me, replacing the harbour and the quay at Killough, the coastguard station and the lighthouse. Gone were the boats and the fishermen, the salvage and the wrack, the sea and the shore. A new life, new friends and new experiences lay ahead.

I had lived all my life in the little fishing village of Killough on the County Down coast. Now, at the age of ten, I was uprooted and transplanted all of seven miles away to the small market town of Downpatrick, county town of Down, with a population of about three and a half thousand. This was an old cathedral city, the centre of a fertile farming area in Lecale that circled round it to the sea. For us, Downpatrick was metropolitan. Killough did not have a town hall, much less one once grandly named the Assembly Rooms, with pointed windows and a carved monogram and a date over the door, and a clock that struck the hour and chimed the quarters. One thing remained constant. We were still going to live in a hotel. Not like the Bangor Arms, our old home, which was really a pub, but a genuine old inn called Denvir's Hotel.

I had been worried about living in English Street among all the English, but my sister Joan had explained that the Irish were there first and had built a church on top of the hill. Then the English, who were really Normans from France, chased them away and built a wall around English Street to keep the Irish out. Then the Irish had to make do with the other hill which was now Irish Street, and other English came and chased the Normans out. Where the Scots came in, she was not sure.

Daddy, who was Downpatrick's town clerk, had an old map, dated 1729, which showed the front of the hotel set back opposite the end of Bridge Street, and the hotel yard. It was in the English Quarter and there was also an Irish Quarter and a Scotch Quarter. The only trouble was that there were five more quarters, named after important public buildings – Market House, Chappell, Windmill, Barrack and Castle – making eight quarters in all. This seemed to me very strange arithmetic indeed. Maybe they counted differently in Downpatrick. What was important, however, as we drove in that first day and stopped to unload the last lorryload of our belongings, was that the hotel was on that old map too.

The hotel, for us, was the centre of life. My mother had bought it at an auction and we moved in on 1 September 1937. It was to be my home for the next thirty years. The hotel had been an old coaching inn going back to the seventeenth century. There was a stone high up in the gable which was supposed to say JOHN & ANN McGREEVY 1642, but it was badly worn and hard to see and it could have said anything. There was a variety of buildings and outbuildings of all types and ages, but none of them modern, on a dozen different levels, all holding out the hope of mystery and adventure as new areas were explored, new doors were opened, and new clean floors were recovered from the engulfing grime.

I arrived on the last lorryload of furniture which pulled up outside the hotel about four o'clock, unable to go through the low arched gateway into the yard until the two tall wardrobes that had been roped standing up behind the driver's cab had been removed. These were pushed through an upstairs window, from which the bottom half of the sash had been removed, by my elder brother Ray standing on the roof of the cab and another man pulling up on a rope from inside the house. Another wardrobe, which was old and painted blue and had been my mother's pride, was sawn in two to get it in and reassembled, but it was never the same again. Eventually, the load lightened, the lorry went into an enclosed yard through a long archway with whitewashed walls from which both whitewash and plaster were peeling off, moss-grown at the bottom and stained quite a way up with horse piss and cow dung. The bed of the lorry was covered with the last detritus of our years of living in Killough, pots and pans and delph in boxes, mirrors wrapped in blankets and laid flat, garden tools, toys and boxes of books.

I doubled back out on to the street and rushed in through the front door for the first time, across the tiled hall and down the steps to a dark and cavernous kitchen where all the others had been working like nailers from early morning. I was made to feel that I had been avoiding the real work, while I believed I had been doing the really important and vital task of securing our withdrawal from Killough, of seeing that nothing was left behind, and of closing that chapter of our lives.

The overwhelming impression of the hotel on that first day was one of grime, of dirt sticking to the floors, of flyblown ceilings, of windows you could scarcely see out through, of mirrors with a scum on them that hid your reflection in shadows, of walls of uniform drab colours, of cobwebs hanging inside every opened door, of cockroaches scuttling into corners in the kitchen and pantry, of greasy tiles and scummy linoleum. There were people trying to get rid of the dirt, a pervading aroma of soft soap and carbolic, buckets of boiling water being carried out, pails of grey stinking suds being poured down the drain, the fetid soapy water having its usual slightly rancid smell, sluiced on its way with cold water from the tap in the jawbox, leaving a dirty rim on the inside of the bucket that had to be swished out separately and wiped clean with a dishcloth. My mother and aunt and Annie Lowry (who had looked after us as infants in Killough and was now pressed into service for the day), and other women were all on their knees with scrubbing brushes and cloths and soft soap and white soap and Sunlight soap, scrubbing, mopping and rinsing. With long-handled scrubbing brushes Ray and another man were toiling away at the floors which started off looking black, covered with lino or some such preparation, then became grey and greyer and lighter until they turned out to be wooden boards after all, and the timber floors began to lend a bit of brightness and character to the rooms. And my older sisters Joan and Claire were hard at work with dusters on the stairs and rubbing walls and windows with damp sponges. And people were carrying in furniture and putting it where Mammy said it should go, and then shifting it again when Auntie Lil gave different orders, carrying in chests of drawers, and taking cups out of boxes and unwrapping lampshades from their newspaper packing and putting them up, and putting light bulbs into sockets and turning them on as the day got darker.

My twin sister Carmel and I skived off from the work, leaving Helen, three years younger, to do the unpacking, and went off to explore. Upstairs to strange endless rooms, over uncarpeted stairs smelling of carbolic and into cupboards smelling of must. We discovered a square cubbyhole with a door, reeking of stale cheese and spilt gravy and rot and decay and putrefaction – this we afterwards learned was mysteriously called a butler's pantry – and a dining room with rickety tables and a drawing room up a flight of steps, and bedroom after bedroom. Out into the yard there were coach houses and stores and a harness room with brackets to put saddles on and hooks to hang bridles and the smell of leather and sweat and oil and horse dung and a rusting, wooden-handled curry-comb lying on the windowsill and a large stiff brush. And a bottling store with racks for bottles and a machine for putting in corks, and piles of old brown oval labels with R. MAGEE or MAGEE'S HOTEL, DOWN-PATRICK, on them, and more dirty bottles and a smell of stale beer and flies and beetles and creepie-crawlies everywhere. The cellar, with great arched brick bins where the stout was laid in sawdust and the wine was kept, was now empty except for a few broken crates, a few half-emptied wine bottles stuck in holes, or half-naggins of whiskey left forgetfully on shelves or furtively behind cupboard doors and now forgotten and forsaken by a drunken proprietor.

Across the yard in a store set into the slanting gable wall beside the steps up to the loft, a vet, they said, had had his shop. Dunlop, they said, whose brother had invented bicycle tyres. The floor was covered with a pile of old medicine bottles, papers advertising patent cures for scour, ringworm, milk fever, felon in cows, hard pad in dogs, wool-ball in sheep and equine diseases such as glanders, strangles, spavin, founder, split fetlock, and others too numerous to mention. Then up a flight of slippery broken flagged steps to a loft with a wooden floor and rafters and beams that seemed to run for ever, and the evening sun flooding in through low windows not much above floor level and gilding the mass of empty boxes and crates and jars and bottles and rusty pots and pans which should have been thrown out and weren't, and concealing the dust and dirt of the floor and making a golden fountain of particles in the sunbeam when disturbed. And bundles of rotting old newspapers covering God knows what holes in the floor, and a trap door which had to be kept clear of in case you fell through, and anyway you were not supposed to be up in the loft where you might get Lord knows what disease, and you should be working with the rest trying to get the place into order. And then across the yard to a large open shed with a carriage in it and two barrel traps, and across a concrete drawbridge, reinforced with two pieces of railway line, into a huge loft with two hearses with glass sides and gilded shafts, better to be got away from quickly, and a brougham for mourners. And down further, looking into the door of the little pig-crew built into the bank, and the horseboxes and the byre and the stables and looseboxes and the large cattle shed and the hay lofts above, and out through the back gate, down the steps, along the side of the cinema, along a narrow cemented passage out into the light again, into the day and the traffic of Market Street. I felt like Robinson Crusoe having walked right round his island for the first time. Now back to the cave to see what could be rustled up for tea.

Tea, the first meal in the new house, was a great

event. Rough and ready it might be as people tired from their labours and laid down their tools, but it had a ritual and a significance about it that were unconscious and unexplained. We all knew there had been a movement of some sort, a shift in location and a change of gear. It was Mammy's great adventure and we all wanted to help her make a go of it. At first, though, we had to find our bearings, to discover what it was we could do to help, and not to be in the way.

The kitchen was down a set of three steps from the inside hall. You came in through the front door to a small hallway with a sliding window of obscured glass opening from the bar, and a flyblown notice calling attention to the limited liability of innkeepers under the Act of Victoria Regina and saying that you could not blame the innkeeper for the loss of your property if you had not given it to him for safekeeping, and in any case you could only claim twenty-five pounds. From the inner hall you could go four ways: sharp right into the little front bar with a polished mahogany counter and shelves with mirrors behind them reflecting bottles and glasses, and other large mirrors advertising Dunville's whiskey and Comber Distilleries and Jameson's, and a clock over the fireplace and a fire and a comfortable settee. Or you could go upstairs, or turn left for the lounges, or down steps and along a narrow passage to the billiard room. Right ahead of you, however, in the middle, the heart of the hotel, was the kitchen with a big dirty black range and a chipped sink in the corner by the window and greasy draining boards and a huge dresser which extended all along one wall from the scullery door to the pantry, with willow-pattern plates set on their sides and great willow-pattern carving platters with little depressions to catch the gravy. In the middle of the floor sat a large deal table with the family all around it and the people who had been working hard all day.

The first night in the new bedroom, the little one over the gateway into the yard: the streetlight mounted beside the window gave light to read by long after the official lights-out, until midnight indeed if you could keep awake that long. As it happened there was little sleep that night because we were soon alarmed by scraping and scratching on the ceiling, under the floor and in the walls. This was soon followed by thunderous bumps on the ceiling as if a hurdle race for greyhounds had been arranged in the roofspace. At first we were terrified, and our fears were not much allayed the next day when James Blaney, to comfort us, said not to worry, it was only the rats. We then discovered that the hotel was right on a rat highway between the rat delights of Thompsons' slaughterhouse on the one side and the equal attractions of Mosey Porter's pigs on the other, with the odd stop in between to pick up refuse from the hotel kitchen. The rats were indeed hurdling over the joists in the ceiling and as they landed on the plasterboard panels above the bed it seemed as if next time they must break through and fall in on top of us.

Daddy went out next day to buy rat traps, springloaded break-back traps that would fracture your hand or foot if you went near them, and large cage traps which were very like the lobster pots the fishermen set in Killough. He fought the battle with the rats for about two years with poison and traps, disappearing through the trap door into the roofspace to set the traps, and reappearing with dead rats to be smuggled to the manure heap out through the back door, or with squealing writhing rats in the wire cage to be drowned quickly in the horse trough in the yard. It took him all that time, and much effort, to block up holes and runs in the walls and under floors, but in the end we were able to sleep easy. It all gave a special edge to 'The Pied Piper of Hamelin' which I was learning off at school, which had the added savour of listing all the wines a good cellar might contain.

As you came up the street just after the town hall clock had struck the half-hour after noon, you might see a small natty man in a swallow-tailed coat with a winged collar and white bow tie, with a clean white napkin folded neatly over his right arm which he held loosely across his front. Silver-haired and silver-moustached, this was James Blaney, the waiter, who added an air of respectability and professionalism to the hotel and at midday liked to stand on the cobblestones sloping up from the front door. He stood so that he could be seen by people at the corner and coming down the street, one leg set forward against the slope, eyeing the passers-by, greeting some as if willing them to come in, fixing others with a stare as if challenging them not to pass by. He said he was attracting business, letting people see that the hotel really was a place where you could expect first-class treatment.

James was very old – he had been working in the hotel since childhood, except for a short period when he had tried to run a place of his own, the Down Hunt (by then the Belfast Bank) in Market Street. He had started work in the still room when he was twelve and worked his way up. He had also worked with several previous owners – Magees, Moores, right back to Denvirs – and he was glad to see the name restored and the place cleaned up and looking like a hotel again. He told of the big room upstairs having been made into one with the ceilings vaulted and plastered and the cornices put in and the folding doors to divide it in two again, all in 1829 to accommodate a dinner at fifteen shillings a head for Daniel O'Connell, who had addressed the crowd in the street below through the upstairs windows, when he came to fight a case in the assizes, and the chair in which he had sat was still in the downstairs sitting room. It was an upright chair, a carver, with a mahogany back rail and two mahogany arms with the seat upholstered in stiff Rexine which was spiky and hairy and scratched the backs of your legs when you sat on it in short trousers. Auntie Lil took it over as a chair fit for a Kerrywoman, and she sat on it for all meals and told us stories about O'Connell, the Liberator, the friend of the people, who was warned by an Irish-speaking servant girl at a great banquet in London not to drink the wine because it was poisoned. But whether she liked the chair because he was a Kerryman, or because it was upright and she liked to sit with a straight back, or because it was uncomfortable and she wanted to do it for the mortification, I never found out.

James said that he was an Irishman, that he had learned some Irish and his real name was Shamus Blanus. He came in every morning about half-past seven to serve the breakfasts, making his appearance already dressed in a clean white shirt and bow tie, needing only to put on his swallow-tail coat. He had a bit of a break in mid-morning before he set up the tables for lunch and took up his station outside the front door. During his break he would unfold the *Irish News* he had brought in with him and left aside in his pantry at the top of the stairs and sit at the fire in the dining room and read his paper. After lunch, when everything had been cleared up and the tables had been reset for the tea, he would take another read before settling down to other tasks such as setting up the tables in the big room for a large dinner or a party. Then you could help him. At other times, the only help you could give was to carry trays up when there was a rush and place them on a dumbwaiter outside the dining-room door, or fill jugs with fresh water, or carry away the trays of dirty dishes and empty glasses. The great privilege of serving at table and addressing the customers, he reserved for himself.

Despite all Mammy's attempts to bring a bit of organisation to the proceedings by introducing dockets that could be filled up as the meal was ordered and presented to customers as a bill at the end, James refused to modernise. He took the orders by word of mouth, memorised them and delivered them to the kitchen himself. Sometimes, especially as he got older, the numbers of guests got confused or the quantities of food ordered were mis-stated or the combinations were mixed up so that the people who got the right soup got the wrong entrée or no dessert at all. In the end, when he was getting a bit dottery, he might order six fillet steaks and trimmings for people who were not there at all or who had died years before. At this early stage, however, he was bright and cheery and dignified and anxious to help my mother to make a go of her venture. He never presented a bill, just announced a total which was by all standards modest enough, and in any case there was not a great deal of variety. There was breakfast, lunch, tea, high tea and dinner and the rates were standard. He was also very particular about change, and gave precise instructions as to how it was to be made up. If you were in the bar when he brought the money down for change he would instruct you never to give him two threepenny bits instead of a sixpence, or a florin when you could give a half-crown. This accounting was based on very practical considerations. James reasoned that a customer faced with the choice between a florin and a half-crown might tip the lesser amount, and there might be some mean-spirited person who would be prepared to tip with a threepenny bit rather than part with a tanner.

James was at his best as a storyteller when you were helping him to clean knives or polish silver. The knives were cleaned in an antiquated knife-polishing machine which was a cylinder like a medium-sized drum, set up on its side on a metal stand and with a handle in the middle for turning, like a hurdy-gurdy. There were slots all round the rim with rubber buffers into which the knives were stuck, right up to the handles. They would have been washed first in warm soapy water: the washer had to be careful to keep the bone handles from going into the water at all because that would soften the cement that kept the tine of the knife firmly anchored in the handle and would make it rocky and unpleasant to use – if it did not fall out altogether. It was important too to put each blade in with the sharp edge against the rubber so that it did not get blunted by the cleaning. Inside the drum there was a series of brushes which whirled round when the handle was turned. There was a vent in the top for feeding in an abrasive cleaning powder, and great fun in whirling the handle around at high speed and making the knives jangle, much to James's annoyance. Actually it was much quicker to use a dab of plate powder and to polish the knives off with a cloth, which, with a little practice, you could do two or three at a time without cutting yourself. Cleaning silver was a much more laborious and boring task, again using plate powder wetted into a paste and smeared on with a cloth or a piece of old newspaper and rubbed off with another before the final buffing and polishing with a clean soft duster. Intricate work required an old toothbrush to get the pink powder out of the mouldings and the whole operation left your hands black and stained and your nose full of the smell of ammonia.

Laying out tables in the big room was another chance to talk to James. First the tables had to be hauled up by Ray; although a smaller boy might stagger up with the trestles one at a time, my brother Ray, who was twice as old as me, could carry four: two over each shoulder. The tables were set up in a pattern to James's satisfaction and covered with white linen tablecloths. The arrangement of knives and forks, plates, spoons and glasses was an art in itself, but the final secret was how to fold the linen napkins so as to make them look like a bishop's mitre standing up in the middle of the place setting. James would talk incessantly about the old days, the coaches and carriages, the looseboxes filled with horses, the hay and straw drawn in to fill the lofts, the harness room filled with tack, the coach for Belfast which left from the yard, and for Dublin by way of Newry, a long distance in Irish miles and an even longer one in English ones. That too was the great age of the county gentleman and the Down Hunt Club, of the assizes which went on for weeks at a time, of the famous murder trials and hangings at the gaol. The commercial travellers would stay for a week with their samples and hired a sidecar to do their visits to the country shops. The commercial room (James's name for the dining room) was reserved for them, and the same faces returned like the swallows year after year until the motor car had displaced the train and the telephone made it unnecessary for people to call at all. James remembered the Boer War and the Great War and the 1918 flu and the Black and Tans and the police barracks in Church Street where the Co-op was, and the Auxiliaries and the B Specials and the problem of being Shamus Blanus while all this was going on.

James said that the recess in front of the hotel between the front door and the boxroom window, which was concreted out to the edge of the pavement and was used as a place for cars to pull in and park, nose to window, tail out over the footpath, was a debtors' sanctuary, a place where you could not be arrested for debt. He said that there was always a sanctuary in churches where people could not be arrested because they were under the control of the abbot, and when the cathedral was in ruins the right of sanctuary was transferred down English Street to the front of the hotel. I asked Mr Johnston, the solicitor, about it and he said it just might be true, but not to rely on it and to pay your debts just in case. James never explained how the person was expected to survive, whether we would be allowed to feed him out through the lounge windows, or whether if he owed Mammy money he could stay there for ever without paying his bill. In any case, nobody ever claimed immunity or put the sanctuary to the test, and we did not boast about it in case it would give people ideas.

TWO

WHEN WE MOVED TO DOWNPATRICK, Daddy and Mammy decided that I should go straight to the secondary school rather than to the Brothers' Primary (as Saint Patrick's Boys' Elementary School was universally known in the town), since I would have to transfer after a year anyhow. This meant that they had to pay for me, and although the fees were small, they amounted to a lot when they were trying to establish a new business and when Joan and Claire were at boarding school and Ray was not yet bringing in a wage. School started the week after we arrived and I found myself in the preparatory class with about two dozen other new boys. Most of them had been in the sixth or seventh class of elementary school and were a year or two older than me, while I had been in fifth class in my old school. As a result, I was put into Prep B, although I was able to go straight into Form 1 at the end of the year.

The new school was very different from the

national school in Killough. For one thing, since we were waiting to move into a new school which was still being built, there was not a proper school building. For the first years school was a room in the Brothers' house, and not always the same room. Sometimes it was the Brothers' refectory and we had to wait until they cleared off after breakfast and get out before lunch. Then the school was run in an adjoining house. Sometimes on good days classes were held in the garden, and sometimes on wet days they took place in the minor hall of the Canon's Hall among card tables and stacked chairs and crates of empty mineral bottles, all smelling of stale smoke and the Sunday night dance.

The Brothers too were different from what I'd known in Killough: old-looking men in long, stained black soutanes with a little white starched square bib at the neck. They were de la Salle Brothers, called after a Frenchman whose picture hung over the mantelpiece in the dining room: BORN RHEIMS 1651, DIED ROUEN 1719, FOUNDER OF THE BROTHERS OF CHRISTIAN SCHOOLS. We had to learn a song about him too, written out in copybooks and bawled off in unison when practising for mass on his feast day of 15 May:

> Saint la Salle, our dearest father,
> To thy children's prayer incline,
> While we sing today thy virtues
> And the glory which is thine.

The Brothers were interesting men, who had been all over the world: India, China, Malaya, America, Singapore, Mauritius, Port Elizabeth. Like the old seafaring men in Killough, they had their tales and their bleached hair, and their skins darkened like mahogany, and their bouts of malaria when they looked awful and were very cranky. Brother David, who had been a lifetime in the East and spoke French and Spanish and dozens of languages you had never heard of, and talked about Joe Louis as if it was pronounced Louee, and Max Schmeling, voiced with a lot of guttural spitting, who beat the Brown Bomber and was beaten back again, and Tommy Farr who in 1937 went the full fifteen rounds with the results of every round being chalked on bogies pulled by pit ponies to bring the news to the miners underground at the coal face in some valley in Wales. And a ship called the *Girl Pat* which sailed away from Grimsby to the South Seas, and Robert Louis Stevenson, whom the Samoans called Tusitala, 'the teller of tales', and a man called Gogan who painted ugly pictures and died of drink and worse. And Wrong Way Corrigan who had set out from New York to fly to San Francisco and landed in Dublin instead.

In the new school there was the strangeness too of a different teacher for each subject, some of them wearing gowns, and classes lasting forty minutes with a bell ringing to mark the end of each period. There was the thrill of new books for every subject, backed by Mammy with brown paper from the roll in Mr Thompson's shop next door – and the new blazer, maroon with gold braid on the pockets and cuffs and a badge with a cross and the words 'Signum Fidei' on it, and a cap to match, and the excitement of new words and new information and new friends and new facts. New questions to ask, new words, new languages. Latin: *mensa, mensa, mensa, mensae, mensae, mensa;* verbs, *amo, amas, amat,* declensions, conjugations, voices, tenses, moods. History and geography in detail never contemplated in Killough.

Brother Wilfrid was the class teacher and he took for English reading books *Hereward the Wake* and *Ivanhoe*. I thought Hereward was a very poor substitute for Cuchulain with little of the magic and none of the tricks. The Fens were all right and the Isle of Ely because it was like the marshes and the Mount, but it was hard to sustain any interest in Saxons fighting Normans for the right to be English. Wilfrid talked a lot about Hadrian's Wall and Stonehenge, but nothing at all about Ballynoe stone circle which you could cycle to in twenty minutes and wonder why the stones were laid out the way they were. Arthur Pollock, the gravedigger, said it was a Stone Age sundial, although it told the years and the seasons rather than the hours and the minutes like the sundial behind Southwell. That was all very hard to believe and Auntie Lil said Arthur often got notions about things. It was probably just a cemetery or something like that.

School was an amalgam of new experiences. There was an avalanche of information, ill-directed and unco-ordinated most of the time, but exciting and stimulating just the same. There were new books to be read, teachers to question again and again until they told you to shut up and get on with your work, there were subjects unheard of, and boys from all over the place and not just one village, each with his story, each with news or gossip, each with a different interest or obsession.

Carmel and Helen went to a different school in the convent, where there were only girls taught, because there was no Catholic girls' secondary school in Downpatrick and they were not ready to go to boarding school with Joan and Claire. By Carmel's account, the nuns were very cross indeed and very strict. One sent Helen home because at the age of seven her skirts were too short, with sheets of newspaper pinned round her going down the street to make her decent; the nun also made Helen sit beside the dirtiest girl in the class because she was too dainty and to punish the sin of pride. As a result she mitched and hid in the chapel until Auntie Lil found her and brought her to school. Mammy was very mad about the newspaper, which she said was a strange one to find in a convent, but when Daddy wanted to go up to give the nun a telling-off, she said not to bother. Carmel soon made her own friends and went to school with them. Although both the girls' school and mine were at the top of Irish Street, I never accompanied them. You would not want to be seen going up the hill with a crowd of girls when the boys were coming up from the train.

At my school there was no place to play but a small cobbled yard which became very full when the big boys came out, some of whom would trip you up and knock you over just for fun. On wet days the big boys gathered under the gateway, while the small boys were pushed out into the rain until the bell rang and we were allowed back into the house where there was warmth and shelter.

On Thursday afternoons, everybody trudged up to a hilly field with goal posts up behind the asylum wall for sports practice. This was so far away that by the time you got there, if you didn't have a bicycle or long legs, it was time to come home again. Not many games were played, and there was little sign of coaching or organised anything.

Soon there was the excitement of preparing for the operetta, for which nothing in Killough had prepared me. The Christmas Rhymers were dismissed as rural crudeness by the town boys, and even the plays in the Hib Hall in Killough did not seem to come up to the mark. The operetta was musical, with a chorus: dramatic, costumed and colourful. We were stepping into a new world. There was the challenge of trying to surpass the triumph scored the previous year by *Once Aboard the Lugger* in which Joey Watters from Ardglass had starred as Chips, the ship's carpenter. This year it was a sickly thing called *The Slave of Araby* about Baghdad with little boys dressed up as slave girls for sale in the market which was very embarrassing when you were sold for a couple of pence, and mooney, sickening songs that nobody would think of singing outside.

> See the hookah's smoke ascending,
> Graceful fragrance soon to die.
> So the hours of youth are wending
> Seize your pleasures ere they fly.
> In Baghdad, in Baghdad, the town of romance,
> In Baghdad, in Baghdad, the pearl of the East,
> Life's one long feast.

Daddy had been in Baghdad during the Great War, in Mesopotamia, although they called it Iraq now. He said the word Mesopotamia meant a land between two rivers, and they were called the Tigris and the Euphrates. He said it was a very nice place, but not at

all as romantic as the song made out, especially in the
bazaar which was dirty and smelly and crowded with
people wanting to cheat you and rob you and pick
your pocket and maybe stick a knife in you if you
were not careful.

Despite the romantic stuff, the people in the play
were splendid, with big boys playing the Caliph, the
Slave Trader and the Captain of the Guard, all in colourful silk robes, with the Captain of the Guard more
splendid than all the rest and waving a piece of ply-
wood cut out to the shape of a scimitar and covered
with silver paper to make it flash in the light.

> See the Captain of the Guard,
> The noble Captain of the Guard,
> The cynosure of every eye.
> And the girls cry out his name,
> For their hearts are all aflame,
> Now the other lovers all are barred.

The new school, of which we were to be the first
pupils, was different again. It was in a field up Saul
Street. Carmel and I went with Daddy sometimes on
a Sunday walk to see how it was getting on. Daddy
said Ned McGrady was a great man who had given
up one of his own fields for the school, only for which
it would not have been possible to get a site for a
Catholic school in the town, and even then it was not
possible to get a proper entrance from Saul Street because the land would not be sold to Catholics. As well
as that, Big Ned had persuaded Lord Dunleath to sell
four acres at the back for a playing field.

The school had been designed by Mr McLean who
used to come out to Killough with Daddy and give us

rides in his car, which Helen nearly crashed one time by pulling on the self-starter and running it over a tree stump on the edge of the footpath. The school cost the enormous amount of fourteen thousand pounds and was being built by Robbie John Hamilton, called 'Staines' because he came from the Ards and spoke with a strong Scots-Ulster accent, and that was how he pronounced 'stones'.

Before the school was officially opened we were all brought up on half-days, when we should have been playing football, to pick up bits of paper and other rubbish from the site. These were stuck to the new tarmac and gathering them meant that tar had to be removed from sticky fingers by rubbing on the grass and then with butter when you got home. Brother Alexis, the headmaster, who was a bombastic little man, was standing in front of the school talking to Staines pointing out all the things he intended to build. The tennis courts would be over there and the swimming pool down below in the corner. Staines, who had probably not yet been paid for the first job, listened as long as he could and then burst out, 'The trouble with you Brither is that ye tak in thusands and ye hae no thusands.'

One day Staines was talking to my mother when a lady in a little Baby Austin car went chugging up English Street. Mammy said he should buy one for his wife, but Staines said it would be like a constipated owl on the road, 'hooting plenty but passing naething'.

The new gymnasium was to be fitted out by a firm from England, and when the school was nearing completion they sent a man over to do the work. He stayed in the hotel, but because he was a tradesman he could not sit in the drawing room with the bank clerks and teachers and commercial travellers who were the regular guests, and so he used to eat downstairs and sit at the fire in our sitting room. Carmel and I tried to cheer him up and make him feel at home by talking in cockney learned from the *Hotspur* and the *Rover*, sprinkling every sentence with 'cor' and "elp' and 'blimey', which we pronounced 'blimmy', until he threw down the newspaper he was reading and told us we had got it all wrong.

The school was opened on Saint Andrew's Day at the end of November 1937. There was a big dinner, which Mammy laid on in the drawing room, with lots of courses and wines, and menus printed on Guinness cards with rhymes like

> Fidgety Phil, he couldn't keep still.
> He twisted, he tangled, and then, I declare,
> Flew into a temper and tilted his chair.

Which everybody thought was very funny since the Brother Provincial, the head of the Brothers in Ireland and Britain, was called Brother Philip. He had come into the class the day before and asked us about poetry and was very cross that none of us knew a poem called 'Don John of Austria' — which I couldn't see why we should be expected to. It must have been his party piece and he went on and on about it.

> Strong gongs groaning as the guns boom far,
> Don John of Austria is going to the war,
> Stiff flags straining in the night-blasts cold
> In the gloom black-purple, in the glint old gold,

Torchlight crimson on the copper kettle-drums,
Then the tuckets, then the trumpets, then the
  cannon and he comes.
Don John laughing in the brave beard curled,
Spurning in his stirrups like the thrones of all
  the world,
Holding his head up for a flag of all the free.
Love light of Spain – hurrah!
Death light of Africa!
Don John of Austria
Is riding to the sea.

It was all nasty, noisy stuff, the way he shouted it out
as if his side was winning, not at all the gentle Richard
Rowley poems Mrs O'Donnell used to read for us in
Killough.

People like him were always a nuisance coming into
a class, showing off and asking questions the boys were
not expected to answer and making the teacher feel
edgy and embarrassed for our ignorance, as if it was
his fault. The worst of all was a priest called the
Ee-Eye who used to come round to examine us on
catechism. He always seemed to pick on a boy who
was slow or who had a stammer or a lisp or a cleft
palate and to keep at the boy until he became red and
tongue-tied and in tears with shame. I thought this
was very cruel, but the bigger boys said not to mind
him, he only came to the school so that he could finish
the day near the golf course: he wanted an excuse to
get playing. Sure enough, if you looked out the back
windows after a bit you would see four black figures
with golf bags and clubs toiling up the hill to the first
green, or searching the whins for a lost ball.

The new school was beautiful. It was so clean that you had to take off your shoes in the morning and wear gutties and put your outside shoes into a little wire basket under your coat peg with its own number down in the cloakroom. Each form had a classroom to itself (which was a big change from the Brothers' house where we were always moving from room to room), with big fixed blackboards and windows looking out over the fields. The corridors were lined with pictures and there was a canteen with a counter and tables with white tablecloths where you could eat your sandwiches if you were staying in, and Mary Connor who had worked in the hotel would give you a bun from the Brothers' table if nobody was looking. You could borrow a bicycle from one of the country boys and ride down the street at lunch time and back up again, but it was better to take a packed lunch and spend the time playing games.

The main game at the school when I started was rugby because Brother Alexis had been in England for a long time and there was Brother Wilfrid who was English and who had been brought over from St Helens to coach the boys. Boys from the Ards and Kilclief played hurley at the side of the rugby pitch; this game was much better if you were small and light and not keen on getting knocked about by bigger boys. The boys from Newcastle tended to play soccer, and you could also play with them on the tarmac with a ball made from brown paper wrapped up tight and tied with twine, but this was frowned on by some of the Brothers because it was not Irish like Gaelic football and by others because it was not classy like rugby.

The nicest thing about the new school was to go up early in the morning before the mist had risen from the valleys. You could look across to the mountains and Cave Hill away behind Belfast and see the tops of the higher hills begin to emerge as if they had been loosely packed in tissue paper, first the tips, then the Fever Hospital and the Workhouse and the Mount and Finnebrogue, with the mist remaining in the hollows until the sun began to shine on the water in the Quoile, and right round to the marshes, and you could begin to see Killyleagh in the distance and Scrabo tower and Shrigley chimney and the streak of silver that was Strangford Lough.

The school played a match in the schools' rugby cup against the Green High, which was the Protestant secondary school at the top of English Street. They were properly called Down High School and we were Saint Patrick's High School, but because of the colour of the school blazers and caps, our school was known as the Red High and they were the Green High. We were all marched up to the game, in blazers and caps, up English Street past the hotel (hoping that nobody was looking out), up Wallace's Lane and through the great granite archway that said DOWN COUNTY GAOL 1834, into the Down High grounds. Under orders to cheer our team on, most of us, especially the younger ones, did not know much about the rules of the game, or what was happening, but we cheered none the less, and in the end our team won narrowly. Next day I heard one of the boys saying that one of their players had called our captain, Johnny Shields, who was the best player on the team, a fenian bastard, which I didn't think was very nice.

Our team did very well after that and got to the semi-final, a match at home against a team called Portora. Joan said this was a swanky school in Enniskillen which was full of people who were going to be army officers and where Captain Oates had gone to school who had gone to the South Pole with Scott and who had walked out into the snow to save the food for the others. Mammy said he shouldn't have been there at all. If they had taken a man from Kerry called Tom Crean, who was a real hero, as strong as a lion, who would not be taken just because he was an ordinary seaman, and only officers could have the glory of getting to the South Pole first although it was the people like Tom Crean who had done all the work. If they had taken him, he would have got them all there and brought them all back, and would not have packed up and wandered off into the snow to commit suicide like Oates.

Anyhow, Oates or not, Portora were a big, strong skilful team and beat our people by a point or two and that was the end of the schools' cup. At the close of the year, Brother Alexis left and the new man, Brother Edmund, changed us to playing Gaelic football. A deputation of older boys went up to the staffroom to plead for rugby while we all stood round and waited. Some of them were county Gaelic players, but they wanted to go on playing rugby at school. They came down very disappointed and reported that he had said it was an Irish school and should play Irish games. There was talk of going on strike or trying to play both, but he would not have that either and that was the end of it. I didn't mind much because I didn't like rugby, but Ray was very cross even though he had left school and had been good enough at Gaelic to play for Down.

One day an Italian Brother arrived called Brother Ubaldo. He was said to be a first cousin of Gigli, a famous tenor whom you could hear on the wireless or on gramophones, and people said that Ubaldo must be a good singer too. He was there as a water diviner, or dowser. He would take a forked stick out of his pocket and walk up and down the hill at the side of the school with the stick grasped in both hands and held out in front of his belly. After a bit it started to wobble and twitch and the point rose up and down spasmodically. He said it was a hazel twig and the twitching showed there was water running underneath the ground. He gave the stick to people to try but it did not do anything for them until he stood behind and caught their elbows and then it twitched a bit. In my case it did not move at all although he pinched my arms quite hard. He took it back again and it twitched some more and he pointed to the spot and said they should dig a well there. This was all necessary because the school was so high up as to be nearly on a level with the reservoir at Samson's Stone, and some days there was no water at all. For weeks after that, the senior boys were digging a shaft with shovels; as the shaft got deeper the boys loaded the soil into buckets, which were pulled up on a rope attached to the handle and the soil was emptied on to a pile at the side. But although the diggers went so deep you could not see their heads and had to lie on your stomach and look over the edge and shout down to tell them about the tea Mary Connor had made, they never found a drop of water and had to fill the hole in again.

I didn't think Ubaldo was a very good singer either, nowhere like as good as John McCormack. Maybe he wasn't Gigli's cousin after all.

The sports day was a big event in the school year with races and jumping and athletics, but most of all there was drill and gymnastics and marching and counter-marching. Boys were divided into their houses, mainly by district, Down, Donard, Quoile, la Salle, each headed by a flag bearer, and there was a colour party with the flags of the houses, green, blue, purple, silver, and the school flag in maroon and gold with the motto Signum Fidei on it and a papal flag in yellow and white with crossed keys and mitre on the white ground. These flags were carried by big boys on ornate heavy poles with tassels at the top, which required a fair bit of strength when the wind caught the large silken flag and blew it out. I used to be commissioned to borrow carrying straps from an Orange lodge, which used the straps to carry the banners every Twelfth of July. This I used to do through my friend Eddie Hayes who was a grocer's assistant in Osfred Hamilton's and who looked after the equipment for the Bells Hill lodge. For all the time I was at school, we used the Orange straps to carry our flags, though surreptitiously, because Eddie could not let it be known that he had lent the property of the lodge to a Catholic school; so each year I returned them, neatly folded and newly polished, in an anonymous brown paper bag smuggled in behind the counter and left on Eddie's bicycle.

The marching and drilling for the sports day required long hours of practice and rehearsal which ate into lunch times and took up every free class for weeks. I remember one practice in particular, which involved Brother Alexis, a fussy, snobby little man who had a number of favourites, all of whom seemed to be boys whose fathers had money or cars or big houses. That day, when we were all out in shirtsleeves, sweating away, Alexis called out a big country boy because he had his braces tied up with string. Alexis exposed him and made a mockery of him before the whole crowd as an ill-dressed lout, despite the fact that the boy had probably been up at six o'clock in the morning to milk the cows before riding six miles on a bicycle to get to school. Then Alexis brought out one of his pets to show how a well-dressed little boy should wear his braces, buttoned up, neatly adjusted, without a hint of binder twine. I thought I should have picked up a stone from the field, or a sod anyhow, and thrown it at him, and I still regret not having done so.

THREE

AT THE TOP OF ENGLISH STREET, PAST THE
courthouse on its high steps, is the Mall,
sometimes called the Mawl, a flat street with
a wide footpath, good for bicycles and skates and our
home-made, four-wheeled gliders, with very little
traffic and few pedestrians either.

To get there you had to pass the grandly named
Mrs Wilhemina McClurg's house, a row of clergy widows' houses set back from the street, and the Masonic
Hall. The houses, each with its own little railed plot in
front, were occupied by elderly ladies who were the
widows of clergymen of the Church of Ireland, or
sometimes their elderly spinster daughters. Sometimes
there would not be enough widows to go around and
a house would be let to a policeman and his family.
The ladies were old and gentle and gracious, and some
of them were very frail, sitting outside like Miss
Olpherts or Mrs Pooler in basketwork wheelchairs on
sunny days. They were always very grateful if you
ran a message for them and might reward you with a

biscuit or a glass of not very fizzy lemonade.

The Masonic Hall was more mysterious and more menacing with the square and compass in plaster over the door, a place of fearful potential. Mammy said would-be masons had to ride a goat before they would be let in and roll up their trouser leg and cut themselves with blades. They had strange handshakes and nods and winks and signs to know each other and they sorted out all the jobs in the courthouse and kept each other right. Running past the door in case a hand would reach out and pull you in and make you ride the goat or worse, you had a feeling of something dark and lurking and God knows what sort of rites or plotting or colloguing going on inside as masons practised their handshakes and their magic words with their aprons tied round their waists. The trouble was that the caretaker was Mrs Love who was warm and decent and cheery and who would give you a cup of tea and could not be associated with any sort of dirty work. Sometimes too we even went to the hall to borrow tables and chairs for functions. Instead of being exotic, it was drab, instead of incense, there was the reek and fug of stale pipe and tobacco smoke, with sometimes the faint aroma of a cigar.

Southwell was a long, low, gracious red-brick building, on the left-hand side, sunk now far below the road, or maybe the road had been raised above it over the years, or maybe it had never been at road level, because if it was, how could the houses on the other side of the street and the barracks be level with the street? Or maybe it was so much older than them that the level had changed in the meantime. Bertie Brown had a picture in his office of the cathedral with an even steeper hill up to it and people wandering about on the muddy road outside the almshouses. Strange, but there Southwell was now, crouching in its hollow, the road level with the eaves and only the cupola sticking up. It was a beautifully proportioned building, one of the nicest in the town if you could only see it all at the one time, which you could not because of the narrowness of the angle and the height of the road. The central gateway, with an arch and cupola, had a small shield with three red rosettes on it and the dates '1733–1933'. Though generally referred to by the neighbours in English Street as the 'almshouses', it was in fact a combination of school and almshouses with a schoolroom at each end and a master's and a mistress's house and sixteen little apartments in between, eight for men and eight for women, separated by the central gateway.

The boys' school was in a big square room at the Masonic Hall end, with a gravelled walled playground around it. At the cathedral end was the house of Mr Smith, the schoolmaster. The large schoolroom at that end had been turned into a store and workshop for him and what had been the playground had been extended to an extensive garden which ran right down to the fence bordering the railway line at the bottom. The old people in the almshouses each had a little plot of land in a series of squares behind the main building. Unlike the front of the building, which was in lovely warm brick, the back was built in a grey, nondescript stone. We thought they were too mean to build it all in stone, like the chapel which was stone all through, even if it was plastered on the inside, or the cathedral, which was built by monks anyhow. It seemed somehow a Protestant thing to do, and all the people in the almshouses were Protestants too. Arthur Pollock put us right and explained that the bricks had been made over in the Inch and that they would have been much more expensive than stone in their day which you could dig up nearly anywhere and use. There were three lovely arches at the back, over little gates on the path down into the garden, and if you tried hard enough, and the light was right, you could line them up so that you could see one right inside the other and the cupola over the main gate at the end. To do that, you had to lie down on the ground flat on your face and lift your head and arch your back and hold that pose for a while. It could be quite sore and it made your knees and hands and clothes so dirty that you could only try it in good weather, but when you could try it, it was worth it.

The people in the almshouses were pensioners and some were very old indeed. Many were fairly active most of the time. I suppose they had to keep going to keep warm. You would often meet them going up and down the street, some stopping from time to time to sit on windowsills, some holding on to railings, some gasping for breath, some reeling from drink, but some brisk and active with a military walk. Many of them were old soldiers who had fought in foreign wars and visited interesting places. One of these was Waffa Brown, who got very argumentative when he got a drink or two. We did not know it then, but he had a strong cockney accent, and his nickname arose because of his cantankerous unwillingness to oblige anyone, and his habit of responding to any request for information or assistance with the almost monosyllabic reply

'Wha' for?' He was a relic of the battalions that had occupied the old gaol on the other side of the Mall when it had been in use as a barracks. He had fought in campaigns on the North-West Frontier and he talked knowingly of Kabul (which he pronounced 'Cobble') and Khandahar. At school, influenced no doubt by Percy French and the necessity to rhyme it with Abdul Abulbul Ameer, we were taught to call it Kabool, and we laughed at Waffa for his ignorance. It was only when, half a century later, the Russians invaded Afghanistan that the BBC confirmed the received pronunciation and reinforced my belief that Waffa had actually soldiered there. Waffa's other great claim to fame, and a probable source of money to buy beer, was as a rat-catcher. Rats abounded and Waffa's services were in great demand at threepence a head, or tail. For sixpence he would catch one with his bare hands. My father said that for a shilling Waffa would kill a rat with his teeth by biting it in the back of the neck. I never saw him do that, and I had no great desire to either.

Another old soldier was Davy McMaster who was local and who got even more paralytic drunk than Waffa Brown. His theatre of operations had been Africa. He had marched with Kitchener to Khartoum and served with Roberts in South Africa. Between them, Davy and Waffa illuminated whole eras of British colonial history, and they helped to restore some of the grime that was lacking from films like *The Four Feathers* and *Beau Geste*. Even from their talk, it was clear that war was much less glossy and glamorous for the Waffa Browns and the Davy McMasters than for the Ronald Colemans and the Errol Flynns.

You had to go down the gravelly path inside the retaining wall and down the concrete steps, along the slippery paving slabs across the front of Southwell if you wanted to get in to Mr Smith's. Mr Smith was not only the schoolmaster; more important, he had a wonderful vegetable garden and you would have to run up to buy a fresh lettuce for the tea, or a cabbage, or peas for the lunch, or to pick redcurrants or gooseberries, big hairy cookers for jams and tarts and nice smooth eaters to be taken on the spot. He had a rich Cork accent, and his wonderful workshop was full of strange old tools and cast-out pieces of furniture which he kept for ever, and desks and blackboards and old maps rolled up or hung on the walls and wheelbarrows and garden implements.

Over the hedge from his garden was the Grove, an area of tall dark trees which ran up to the wall of the cathedral graveyard. The ivy in the undergrowth was full of rats and, we feared, snakes, adders and serpents too, although if Saint Patrick had banished the reptiles from Ireland as they said and we fervently believed, he had surely got rid of them from his own graveyard where he was buried himself. In the middle of the Grove there was a stone that said that John Wesley had preached there one hundred and fifty years before. Carmel said he was a preacher who was not a priest and not to bother with him or even to read his stone as it might be a sin and he was like the people who used to put up tents in Montgomery's field, or Minnie Martin's meadow, or the Cooneyites. Anyhow it was a queer place to preach when the cathedral was close beside him, and very hard for the people to see him with all the trees and ivy.

It was also the place where the crows came in the evening, homing in from all points of the compass, heaving and squabbling, a whirling mass against the clouds and a darkening sky, creating a dreadful noise before settling down for the night.

The Grove was where Bertie Brown planted his flowers every year. When Dicksons and Kellys and the other merchants were clearing out their stock, he used to get them to give him all the unsold daffodil bulbs and he would plant these under the trees. You could see him, a tall thin man with a wintry sort of timid smile, a brown paper bag of bulbs in one hand and a long stick – a spade handle with a sharpened point on one end – which he stuck into the ground with the other. This made a broad round hole about six inches deep into which he dropped a single bulb. If you were quiet and did not make too much of a nuisance of yourself he would let you hold the bag of bulbs, or maybe drop one into the hole – so long as you kept the hairy side down and the pointy bit up – and sometimes, even, you could gather old leaves from the ground and use them to fill up the top of the hole so that the frost would not kill the bulb or the water drown it or the rats scrape it up and eat it.

In the spring the daffodils came out, a beautiful yellow carpet under the trees, and clumps of bluebells too, and everybody said how good Bertie was, and it was a sin to pick the flowers and you never did. But at the end of the month when the flowers were withering, Bertie would pick some and give them to people he liked or who he thought deserved them. He always gave my mother a bunch, which pleased her very much: nothing ever said, no fuss, just a small bunch left on the hall table inside the open door, no note, no anything, but Daddy always said, 'It's your boyfriend again.'

Bertie worked in the Dunleath Estate office and was the Steward of the Southwell Charity. He knew every field and ditch and boundary wall in the Demesne of Down, as it was called, and he had lots of interesting old maps hanging on the walls of his office. The children had a rhyme about him:

> Who are the finest pair in town?
> Eva Pratt and Bertie Brown.

Eva Pratt lived in Scotch Street and had a millinery shop in Market Street with a couple of flyblown ladies' hats on little wooden stands in the window. I don't think there was any reason to connect her with Bertie Brown except that they were both tall and thin and their names fitted the rhyme.

Some called the people in the almshouses paupers, but I thought this was a nasty name. They were not in rags, they did not beg, they were nice kind gentle old people, except for one or two. Some of their plots at the back of Southwell were wild, others had been dug. Some people used them to grow vegetables, others just sat there in the sun. There was a gate at the bottom out on to the path which led along the railway line to the Grove. Outside this gate, across a muddy path, was a fence made of sleepers hammered into the ground but overgrown and festooned with brambles and ivy. On the other side of this, seen through the cracks at ground level, or over the top from higher up the hill, was the back of the railway station and the gleaming lines where you could not go at all without being killed by a train. The trains came in slowly from the direction of the loop line and disappeared behind a brick wall as they slithered to a stop at the platform. But sometimes, if you waited, you could see the engine pull out on its own at the other end of the wall and inch on to the turntable. This was a narrow iron platform with rails on it and railings along the sides, balanced over a round hole in the ground with a retaining wall around it. The engine got on to the turntable and stopped with a great hissing of steam being released. Then two men would push a handle at the end of the railing and the whole thing would swing slowly round like a clock being wound, or like the horse-thresher in James MacMahon's haggard. Ever so gently the great engine, quiet now and burping only occasional snorts of steam, would swing round until it was facing in exactly the opposite direction and the rails on the platform were lined up again with the rails on the ground. Then the man would shout, 'Right. Take her away', and the engine would hiss a bit and bang and grunt and groan as she set off in the opposite direction, this time on the outside track and on the side of the wall nearest to us, and then move off smartly and without burden in the direction of the loop line. And the engine would give a little hoot and look light and free as if it were glad to be rid of the carriages and wagons for a while, like a foal frisking across a field away from its mother, but not too far away in case it got lost. And down at the signal box it would stop again, Paddy Blaney would lean out the window to make sure everything was all right before pulling the levers to change the points. The engine would then reverse into the station until it banged into the carriages and shook them – and you could see the buffers going in a bit and coming out again – and then there was a clatter of chains as the engine was hooked up to the train once more and the hoses were connected and she was ready to go off back towards Belfast or Newcastle or Ardglass and Killough.

Sometimes in the winter there was water all over the tracks and up to the fence and over the path and across the bottom of the garden; then the train would come in as slowly as you like, but still sending a great surge of water like the bow wave of a ship, right out against the fence and breaking in splashes up against the brick wall on the far side. And the people in the shops and houses in lower Market Street, opposite the station, Skeffingtons and Kellys and Reas, would get out their planks and boxes and barrels as the flood water welled back up the gulley-grates, so they could not get neither out nor in their front doors, and it invaded the downstairs rooms that were on a level with the street. But most of the people had raised the floors of their downstairs rooms, and used planks to provide a series of gangways from the crown of the road into each shop. Then we would all cry:

> The floods are up in Market Street,
> The station's like a shore,
> And Paddy Kelly's glad to hear
> It ain't gonna rain no more.

On the other side of the Mall from the almshouses was the old gaol, known interchangeably as the barracks but now closed up and locked with a great wooden gate that you could look in through the cracks of and a small wicket in the middle that opened sometimes, but not often. There was a German gun outside, a howitzer, Daddy said, captured in the war and brought there as a trophy to remind people who had won. I thought he might have captured it himself but he said no, it would have come from France where he had not been, and anyhow he did not go in for capturing guns and he would have left it where it was if he did, and it was a silly thing to bring it there in the first place, and the war was over and don't be raking all that up again, and the Germans had more guns of their own now and Hitler was an awful man and there would be another war before long and it would be far worse this time, he would say. Still, the old gun was a great curiosity and good for climbing over and swinging off the barrel and sitting on the meshed seat as if you were in charge, enfilading the trenches, mowing down dervishes with grapeshot, or stopping the Light Brigade in their tracks.

Outside the barracks was a high stone wall with no openings in it except the gateway. The barracks had been the headquarters of the South Down Militia, the terrors of the land that Davy McMaster used to sing about on a Friday when he got his pension and had a pint or two. Before that it had been a gaol; some people called it the old gaol because there had been a newer gaol round the corner where the Down High School was now. There was a bricked-up opening over the gateway of the old gaol with a piece of iron sticking out. Artie Pollock said that was where they used to hang people. He said they hanged a man from Cork there called Thomas Russell. I asked Mr Smith if he knew him, but he said he didn't, he had left Cork a long time ago, and he was a silly man to do what he did and not to bother about him. Joan said he was silly because he had started a revolution and had been given away by informers out at the Buck's Head. People who started revolutions in Ireland were always let down or given away and it was better not to bother at all.

Later in school I had to learn a piece of a big long poem to recite at the concert:

> By Downpatrick gaol I was bound to fare
> On a day I remember, feth,
> For when I came to the prison square
> The people were waitin' in hundreds there
> An' you couldn't hear stir nor breath!
> For soldiers were standing, grim an' tall,
> Round a scaffold built there foment the
>   wall,
> An' a man stepped out for death!
>
> I was brave an' near to the edge of the throng,
> Yet I knowed that face again.
> An' I knowed the set an' I knowed the walk
> An' the sound of his strange up-country talk,
> Then he bowed his head to the swinging rope,
> For he spoke out right an' plain.
> Then he bowed his head to the swinging rope,
> Whiles I said 'Please God' to his dying hope,
> And 'Amen' to his dying prayer,
> That the Wrong would cease and the Right
>   prevail,
> For the man that they hanged in Downpatrick
>   gaol
> Was the man from God-Knows-Where!

I could never go up to the Mall after that without seeing the crowds around the gate, spilling down the hill into English Street, and hearing the quiet as they waited for the rope to stop swinging.

Artie said they had brought the body round the back of the courthouse and down the lane to Bridge Street where there was a gate in the wall and steep steps down into the parish church graveyard. He said if you looked hard and lined up the second window of the Co-op with the trunk of a tree in the graveyard and walked along the line they made and felt with your feet until you found the bump and then pulled the grass away, you would find a flat stone marked THE GRAVE OF RUSSELL, 1803. He said it had been put there by Russell's friend Mary Ann McCracken whose brother had been executed for leading the '98 Rebellion. I thought she might have been a relation of Willie McCracken, the carpenter who had made the cart I had in Killough, but Artie said no. Oddly enough, he made coffins too.

On the upper side of the old gaol were two bow-fronted houses, called the Judges' Lodgings, with old people living in them. One was Mr W.O. Martin, a very old retired bank manager who used to come out in his dressing gown and sometimes wore a brown shoe with a black one, or came down the street to the shops in his slippers and a long overcoat trailing the ground and a little wickerwork carrying bag. He sometimes rode a very old bicycle which he rode up the hill with no gears, standing up out of the saddle and pressing on the pedals until he got up to the flat part just beyond the courthouse. Apparently it was one of the first Raleigh bicycles ever made and he had kept a log to show how often he had ridden it, and how many miles, all over the place. When it was fifty years old he sent the log to the makers and they sent him a lovely new bike with three-speed gears, cable brakes, a dynamo and everything. Strangely though, he did not ride this one up English Street, but got off at the bottom of Bridge Street and pushed it the rest of the way, leaning in against the handlebars until he got to the flat. Daddy said Mr Martin was getting old. One day he said to him, 'The hill is getting steeper, Mr Martin.' Mr Martin replied crossly, 'It's not that. It's these new bikes, the chains are not as strong and the sprockets will wear out.'

Below the old gaol the courthouse stood high above its steps with a statue over the pediment that had a sword in one hand and a scales in the other. Daddy said it was Justice, what the law was supposed to be about, even-handed, balanced like the scales, and handing out punishment with the sword. The scales were badly tilted to one side, but then the sword was broken too so I supposed that evened things out.

At the side of the steps, reached through a wrought-iron gate in the railings, was a round screen of cast iron about six feet high with an intricate pattern of holes in it. Behind this was a public lavatory or, more precisely, a men's urinal. There were no doors on it, the curtain of iron was all that hid what was going on inside from the view of passers-by. Claire said that in France the screen would be only half the height and men could raise their hats to ladies going past on the street while they did their business. I thought that was an odd way to go about things. Every time Daddy saw the public lavatory he told his story about the councillor who wondered why, if the council could provide urinals, they could not build arsenals as well.

Next below the courthouse was the Down Hunt Club which Arthur Pollock said had been a gaol, an even older gaol than the old gaol, where people were kept sometimes for years until they paid their debts, and others were kept for a short time until they were hanged up on Gallows Hill, at the back of Scotch Street, which you could see towering behind the town hall steeple, with the great gash cut in it where the road went up. He said the gallows was built on the flat bit of ground like a platform behind Ned Williamson's house and the men waiting in the prison to be hanged, often for small things like stealing a sheep, could see their friends being executed. Artie had a newspaper cutting headed 'Believe it or not . . .' which told how one man had tried to escape from being hanged. His friends had an iron collar made, supported by straps around his body. The collar was hidden by a scarf so that the hangman did not see it when he put the rope on. This was to prevent the condemned man from being choked when the noose tightened, and to take the weight of his body without pulling his head off. The plan was that he should feign death until his friends returned in the night to cut him down and take him away. They would bring a coffin full of stones and bury it, pretending he was in it. Unfortunately the straps rubbed against his balls and he could stand the pain no longer so he started to twitch long after he was supposed to be dead. The soldiers saw him and cut him down and next day he was hanged again, this time without the collar and with the scarf taken off so that the hangman could see his neck. According to Artie's cutting, it was made the rule after that that the hangman had to bare the victim's neck. It all reminded me of the tableau of the Stations of the Cross in the chapel with the soldier sticking his lance into Christ's side. With this sort of information, I was never very keen to go up the Gallows Hill in the dark.

The Down Hunt Club opened officially on a couple of days each year but sometimes the door was left open and Freddie Haines, the caretaker, would let you creep in over the cold, stone-flagged floor into the dank corridor and up the stone stairs to a room with a large polished mahogany dining table. The walls were hung with drawings and paintings and photographs of men's heads, hung one above the other in family groups, some of them cartoons and caricatures. These were all members of the hunt over the years, which was the oldest in Ireland and started the horse races out at the Old Course. You could follow the family features like a big nose or buck teeth or a fat head from grandfather to father to son. Sometimes Freddie would take you into a smaller room and open a cupboard and take out a couple of chamber pots, delph po's with a man's head painted on the bottom on the inside. Daddy said he was Gladstone, a great man who had cut down rents and broken the power of the landlords and favoured Home Rule so that the grandees hated him and wanted to piss on his face to show their contempt.

Next to the club, on the top floor over a set of very Dickensian offices, was Miss Munce's school, to which were sent the children of rich Protestants who did not think the Southwell schools were good enough for them.

The cathedral hill at the top end of the Mall was the

first centre of the town and the reason for it being there at all. As you went up the hill from the Mall you passed a weather-beaten Celtic cross where the road divided to go round the two sides of the cathedral. The figures on it were barely visible. It had once been the town cross down at the bottom of the street, and the base had been used as a horse trough down in the hotel yard before it was recovered and the cross was re-erected. Behind the cross was a door which Carmel said could not be opened because when the Protestants stole the cathedral from the Catholics and drove out the monks, the monks locked the door and took the key away with them and threw it into the waters of the Roughal halfway across to Inch Abbey where nobody could ever find it and the door had remained locked ever since and they had to make another door at the other end of the cathedral to get in. But if the Catholics ever got the cathedral back, the key would float to the surface and be found and the door could then be opened again.

It was good to know this – but a great disappointment to come up one day and find a little wicket in the middle of the great door lying wide open; peeping fearfully inside in case a dead and forgotten monk was letting himself out, I found old Mrs Pollock, the verger, Artie's mother, pottering about inside with buckets and mops.

At the side of the cathedral up a couple of steps and along a gravel path was a large flat stone with a chip out of the side and a cross and the name PATRIC cut in the top. This was Saint Patrick's grave where he was buried along with Saint Brigid and Saint Colmcille so that we could recite

In Down one grave
Three saints do fill,
Patrick, Brigid and Colmcille.

Old Mr Maguire the painter said the stone had been put there by a man called Bigger from Belfast who had restored Shane's Castle in Ardglass. Mr Maguire remembered it being hauled in from the quarry at Ballymagreehan on a low cart drawn by teams of horses along the Vianstown Road. Stream Street was too steep for the horses so they had to go round by the Circular Road and Market Street. The stone was solid granite and it weighed tons. Arthur Pollock had a wicked story that it was not Saint Patrick's grave at all but the family grave of a barber who had made fun of a cathedral sexton by shaving off half his beard. In order to get his own back, the sexton took to pointing out the barber's family grave to strangers as the resting place of Saint Patrick. Then it became a place of pilgrimage so that the barber dared not be buried in it. Artie said the pilgrims began to carry away bits of soil as relics and the grave was getting dug out, so Bigger put the slab on it with PATRIC carved on the top. Artie said Downpatrick had been an important place long before Saint Patrick's time. If not, Patrick would not have come there to set up his church. Auntie Lil said it was a good laugh but not to listen to everything Artie said since he was a bit of a joker and a Protestant and probably not very keen on Saint Patrick. Joan said that Down was marked on an old map made by a Greek man called Ptolemy; maybe there was something in what Artie said. Auntie Lil said it was still rubbish, and dangerous rubbish at that.

What would we do if the tourist buses did not come to visit Saint Patrick's grave?

The other graves around were far more interesting, overgrown with ivy and with toppled headstones and broken slabs and mouldy inscriptions that you had to spit on your finger and rub before you could read them, and even then it was difficult. One was all in Irish about the Uí Laithbheartaigh (the O'Lavertys) of Lecale and another was a broken vault where you could squint in through a hole and claim to see skulls and bones and bits of coffins and scare all the others away. In the evening the crows came with a rush of wings and a great cawing to circle before roosting in the trees of the Grove where they had their nests year after year. Further on in the new graveyard you could stand at the fence and see right across the marshes to Hollymount with the Mourne Mountains changing colours in the background. If they were dark blue it was going to rain, green was fine all the time. Sometimes they seemed to be miles away, other times very near, sometimes with clouds covering the peaks, other times with rain slanting down like hatching on a picture. Arthur Pollock said you should try to imagine the view the way it was when the old Celtic chief built his house on the hill and fortified it, all surrounded by water and the other hills covered with trees and sticking up above the water. Down to the left just beyond the loop line you could see a mound with four trees which was the grave of Magnus Barefoot, King of Norway. Good enough for him too, trying to attack the cathedral and rob the poor monks saying their prayers. He should have stayed in Norway where he would have been safe.

Just over the fence the ground was very uneven with humps and hollows and trenches all around. Daddy said it was a mass grave where the cattle were buried that were slaughtered in an outbreak of foot-and-mouth disease, and he knew everything. But Artie said it was the remains of a Celtic fort that had been built on the hill, and you could see the outline of the rampart if you went out the Ballydugan Road and looked up against the light. He said that people had been living there for four thousand years and we were very lucky to be allowed to live there too. He said there was treasure in the mound and one day he was going to dig for it and find it. I preferred Artie's story to Daddy's, but I didn't like to say so. Maybe they were both right.

The cathedral was a place apart. You couldn't go in there when there was a service on because that would be a sin – and they wouldn't like it much either. But to creep in out of the sunlight when the door was open and old Mrs Pollock was cleaning the place was very tempting and maybe not much of a sin at all. It smelled very musty as if nobody ever went in, and damp and cold and dark and not like the chapel where there was always a lamp and God was there all the time. There was a great granite tub which was used for christenings, which had also been a trough in the hotel yard, and tattered flags hanging from the rafters and coats of arms on the walls and wooden boxes with benches instead of proper seats. Sometimes you could hear Albert Coulter practising on the organ, which sounded beautiful, but he was a cross old man and you had better not let him catch you.

The organ was mounted on an arch between the porch and the main part of the cathedral where the seats were and the wooden pew boxes. When Mr

Coulter played, it filled all the space with a wonderful rich sound. Artie said that the organ had come from Windsor Castle and had been made by a very famous organ builder called Greene. He said the king had been mad to give it away, but he was mad anyhow and had given America away too.

Arthur lived with his mother in a red-brick bungalow which had been built for the verger. He knew more about everything than anybody but Daddy, and he even knew some things about old stones and graves and things in the ground and who had been living on the hill and what they did that Daddy was not so sure about. Arthur could look at a stone and tell you what wall it came out of and what quarry, and how it was cut, and show you a couple of scratches on the end and say, 'There it is. That's the Norman mason's mark. The same man worked at the building of Inch Abbey. He must have been a monk.' He could read stone walls the way other people read books and he could look at the land and strip away hedges and fences and tell you what it looked like hundreds of years before and where the roads went and where the mooring places and the piers and bollards were for the boats that used the river and how the water came right round the hill and made it nearly an island so that de Courcy could build a wall across the bottom of English Street 'from sea to sea' and cut the street off from the rest of the place.

At the bottom of English Street was the town hall, which dominated and defined the centre of the town. It was a gentle sort of dominance because it was a quiet building which did not shout its presence. Indeed the only noise it made was the striking of the clock which was very erratic, likely not to be on the hour and not to give the proper number of strokes anyhow. The tower had a clock dial on each of its four sides and each told a different time, which was awkward if you were running back to school and the Irish Street face was ahead of the time showing towards English Street. If Mammy did not like someone, or distrusted them, or thought they had tricked or deceived her in some way, she would dismiss them as having 'more faces than the town hall clock'.

On the corner of the building near the main door there was a granite milestone bearing the legends *Cwellan 9* and *Newry 24*. The distance to Newry seemed short until Daddy explained that it was given in Irish miles which were longer than English miles because the Irish perch was longer than the English perch and the Irish acre was bigger than the English acre. He showed me the tables on the inside of the cover of the old school jotter which we had learned off by heart: five and a half yards one perch pole or rod, forty perches one furlong, eight furlongs one mile. The difference was that the Irish perch was seven yards which could only have been because Irish men were bigger or had a longer stride or could run faster than Englishmen.

The town hall corner, with the red-brick hall and Ben Logan's chemist's shop (chiropody half a crown a foot: Ray said that meant seven and six a yard) with Massa Johnston behind the counter, was where English Street met Irish Street and Scotch Street. There was no Welsh Street. I wondered why. Years later I read a poem by Roy McFadden who argued

> The Welsh, having Saint Patrick,
> Needed no street.

FOUR

SOON AFTER WE ARRIVED IN DOWNPATRICK,
Daddy bought a cow which enabled him to re-
visit his roots and pretend to be a farmer again
as he milked her night and morning. It was a gentle
little roan shorthorn which he bought from Mr
McGrady and we called her Millie after a character in
the *Dandy*: Millie the Million Gallon Milker. The old
byre was cleaned and scrubbed out and whitewashed
and hay was brought in and forked up to the loft and
tramped down and stored, and straw for bedding. I
was up in the loft receiving the hay, warned to look
out for the tines of the pitchforks, careful not to slip
or fall or impale myself upon them which would be
fatal, and charged too with looking out for damp bits
of hay which would heat up and maybe cause a fire in
the middle of winter, and all the time tramp, tramp,
tramp until legs are sore and tired, but it is an important job to pack it all in and get it tight and solid and
without air holes and fit for Millie for the winter when
she would have little grass to eat, would maybe not

get out at all for days on end, but a few wisps of hay and a bucket of bran mash, made with boiling water at the kitchen sink, covered with a sack and brought down when it had cooled a bit. The old house across the yard, which had been Dunlop the vet's office, was cleaned out of old medicine bottles and the dirt of ages was scraped off the floor and the flags were scrubbed with carbolic and the walls were whitewashed and the windows were taken out and replaced with wire screens to make a cool room for the milk to sit in shallow enamel basins and not go sour even in the warmest weather.

Then a field had to be rented behind the old gaol, down a little lane leading to the Mount, past Fanny Breen's garden. The field itself was about four acres, three Irish, Daddy said. It sloped down from the back wall of the old gaol to a broad drain, across which was the marshes. It was full of thistles which had to be pulled out by the roots with a pair of large wooden-handled tweezers before the seeds scattered and Daddy was prosecuted by the police for not cutting them. Mammy said it was all a matter of taste. Thistles were quite beautiful things in their own way: flowers whose time had not yet come. The Scots thought a lot of them just as we did of the shamrock. That did not seem to impress the police and so hard days were spent and fingers were prickled getting rid of the blooming thistles. Worse still was the yellowboy or ragwort which grew rank and rife and had to be scythed down before it could do more damage. It left such an awful smell on the hands, even after scrubbing, that it was no wonder it was called 'stinking Willie'. So too the clumps of fierce nettles which stung the legs off anybody in short trousers, leaving white and reddening blisters on all exposed skin, which then had to be massaged by dockens to ease the sting. Only Daddy could use the scythe; he settled into the rhythm he had learned in his youth and mowed down the nettles with wide and easy sweeps, stopping every now and then to rest the point of the scythe on the ground and to sharpen the blade with a stone wetted in water.

The great thing about the field was that it gave access to the old gaol from the back: over the wall, through an overgrown garden plot and into the main building by way of a gaping hole in the wall, then into the old cells with the vaulted roofs where the convicts had lain before being transported to Van Diemen's Land, and into the space around the Governor's House and the guardhouse at the gate. Best of all, in the front corner, the wall had been plastered and the floor had been laid out in concrete to make a handball alley. It was an unusual shape with only one side wall, but the floor was true and unbroken and you could play away all day without anybody seeing you. If you got tired of handball or were on your own, you could practise hurling with a tennis ball, beating it against the walls and meeting it on the volley as it flew unpredictably out of the angle of the corner. It was our secret: only we had the key and the way in and we kept it to ourselves.

After a while, we got another cow called Angeline, because Millie could not keep the supply up all year, going dry for a period before calving. Every now and then the cows would break out and canter off across the marshes or into neighbouring fields and they had to be chased and found, us and them ploughing across drains and in and out of sheughs or through broken barbed-wire fences or through gaps in thorn hedges. Sometimes they got very restless: then they were said mysteriously to be 'on the country'. Tommy McQuoid the cow-doctor would then be sent for to bring them to Bohills' bull which spent most of its time ferociously guarding its herd in the field around the Mount. Before the cows calved, Daddy fed them with spoonfuls of brown sugar in their bran mash to ward off milk fever which would cause them to collapse and die, and there was always the application of archangel tar to teats and udders to prevent felon, and numerous other ailments which had to be treated by Tommy McQuoid who was better than any vet.

When the cows became too much for Daddy to look after on his own, Frankie McCrissican was hired as a yard boy and general help to look after them, and then to learn the bottling of stout and beer and everything else about the hotel. And as the business grew further and the demand for milk with it and the need to cover periods when one or other cow was dry, Daddy decided to buy a third. He took me with him in a taxi along with Ned McGrady to a farm at Bright, out behind Áine's grave, to old Dick McIlmail who for thirty pounds sold him a beautiful red cow which had just calved. Thirty pounds was a huge price at the time, but it was the war by then and prices had been driven up. There was much looking at teeth and into eyes, and patting of rumps and feeling udders and weighing the bag in their hands and feeling the straightness of the back and the set of the head and the spread of the bones where the calf had been delivered, and examining the swish of the tail and the sheen of the coat. And Mr McGrady said it was a fine animal, if a bit on the dear side. And Daddy said, 'No point in spoiling the ship for a ha'porth of tar.' So the deal was made, Mr McGrady splitting the difference, and five shillings for a luckpenny and two pennies for me to buy sweets and the cow was to be walked the five miles to her new home.

In a week she was dead of milk fever, despite the efforts of Mr Lawther, the vet, which was another expense. The strength left her legs and she fell down and rolled over on her side and got weaker and weaker and died. Mammy was very sad at the loss of the money, and cross with Mr McGrady for having advised Daddy to buy, and with Daddy for paying so much, and mad with Dick McIlmail for having sold us a sick cow. She said it just showed you should never do business with a friend. Daddy said Dick must not have fed her with brown sugar. A spoonful a day would have done, or treacle at a pinch.

Going for the cows was an opportunity to practise hurling with an ashplant and an old boot polish tin, up and down the street keeping clear of cow clap and streaks of runny shite; you went slow going up and coming down with the cows, careful not to let them run and jiggle the milk out of their teats when their udders were full. Calving involved sitting up all night, sometimes in the byre with a hurricane lamp waiting for the cow to begin and then running up to rouse Daddy. There would have been comings and goings all day and Daddy and Tommy McQuoid looking at her and feeling her udder for tightness and her rump to see if the bones were dropping as the cow readied herself for calving. Then an attempt to guess when she would do it, which was nearly always too late or too early which left the watcher in a panic and ensured the need to run madly for help when she finally decided to move. Daddy would run down and Ray and Tommy if he was there and sometimes, if there were complications, Mr Lawther who generally brought his sons with him, so there could be quite a crowd in the byre. Generally, however, the cow did it by herself, with very little assistance except that the calf had to be rubbed with straw and pulled round to its mother's head to be licked before it got up on spindly legs to nuzzle her. Daddy would draw some milk off to ease the pressure on the udder, 'stribbing', he called it. You could not drink the beestings, but the calf could. After that there was the calf to feed with milk in a bucket, using your fingers to get it to drink and being cut in the shins by the rim at the bottom as the calf bucked and rattled the bucket with its head.

When milk was scarce, it was up to Bohills' dairy for supplies; Bohills' was in Bridge Street, a strange wonderland which got more exotic the further up you went. There were crowds of boys who looked as if they might beat you up, although they never did, or shouted at you and threw stones when you were bringing in the cows, yelling strange hurtful insults, 'Your mother's a tinker. She came to the town begging. My da knows.' Most of the time the Bridge Street residents were quieter people, who took the short cut through our yard to Market Street, although the gate had to be locked at night to prevent it becoming a right of way. The houses too were different, some of them with big Union Jacks hung out of low upstairs windows for the Somme and Remembrance Day and the Twelfth of July and other times, and some of the door and window surrounds painted red, white and blue.

At the botttom of Bridge Street, really in English Street, was Bob Watterson's barber's shop. Bob always required chat and talk from his customers, but he would take neighbours first even if there were others waiting. It was better, though, not to get out of turn and to sit and hear the chat. Mostly it was Mr Cochrane talking about shooting and pheasants, and when the greylag geese were due on the marshes and when they left and where they came from in the Arctic Circle and where they were going to in Africa, and how the marshes were the centre of the wild goose universe as they flew from the North Pole to the South, and how Captain Scott (who did not get to the South Pole) had a son called Peter who came and painted birds on the marshes. The Cathedral Marsh was the most important bit of all.

Once, to make conversation in the chair, I told Mr Watterson about seeing two crows fighting over a crust in the school playground when another, bigger bird came and knocked them away and took the crust. Was that a hawk or a corbie or a carrion crow? Mr Cochrane came in before I was finished and Bob told him about it and I had to go over the whole thing again in great detail. Mr Cochrane got very excited and said that only a golden eagle was big enough and fierce enough to do that and one had not been seen in Ireland for a hundred years and maybe he should go straight home and write a letter to the *Field* and I was an observant little boy who would be a great naturalist one day. I was getting very worried about this because whilst the crows descended in flocks on the gravelled playground immediately after lunch each day, there had been no other bird, no corbie, no hawk, certainly no golden eagle. But my lie kept sucking me in as Mr Cochrane asked for detail and I had to strike out wildly. Maybe it wasn't as big as all that, maybe just another crow, or a jackdaw, or a hooded crow – weren't they bigger than the others? – and maybe it hadn't knocked them over, maybe it was just the wind and he stole the crust. It was far away anyhow, out through the window, and it all happened in a flash, and maybe we had better wait to see if it returned before writing to the papers.

On the other side of Bridge Street, behind Miss McIlroy's fine big square brick house on the corner where she made superior dresses for superior ladies, in a little yellow-washed house Mr Galbraith made tin cans and vessels and repaired all sorts of metal things. A man of precise craft and skill, he made a special funnel for Mammy to make black puddings with and gallon cans. He sat on a stool in the small space between the fire and the window so that he had light from one and heat from the other, tap-tapping away, clip-clipping the tin, the floor covered with scraps, the soldering irons stuck between the bars of the range, ready to hand as he greased on a drop of flux with a forefinger, bent the rod of pliable solder with one hand, held the point against the joint, the vessel held between his knees, and seared it with a soldering iron. Then a dip in a basin of water, a rub with an oily rag and the gallon can was ready to be brought home to Mammy to be scalded in boiling water before being used for the milk.

Further up the street, Bohills' cows wandered into

the yard from their fields around the Mount having come down the stony lane from the gaol wall. Inside the open yard gate, through the open door of the dairy, you could see the coolers and sterilisers and racks of bottles, and Paddy Bohill hosing down the floors and walls, water whitened with milk running down the drain before he loaded up the crates on his flat cart, whipping up the cob and going off on his rounds as he did every day, morning and evening.

The houses in Bridge Street were low, generally with half-doors, with women and men leaning out over the bottom half shouting gossip up and down the street or calling the children. At night all doors were closed, so one night an open door caused disaster for one happy old fowl merchant. With bad legs and a good drop taken, on a Saturday night he would square himself by Bob Watterson's window and navigate from there by placing the flat of his hand against the wall, moving one foot at a time, keeping the wall at arm's length up the hill and home, missing the pump and the jutting-out steps until he came to his own gateway where he collected and sorted eggs and brought fowl home and killed and plucked them. One night somebody left a door open halfway up the street, and in the dark our man, finding a hole where there should have been solidity, fell heavily into the inside hall, shaking himself nearly sober.

Jimmy Dick lived in Bridge Street; he was a knacker, who bought dead animals and carted them off. A big, big man, he could roll a cart wheel up the street with one hand, or reach up to catch a child who mocked him through an upstairs window and frighten him. But he was a gentle giant. Later on, in the war, his son was in the army when Rome was liberated and he met the pope. Jimmy told Mammy about this in the yard one day, and said that his son thought that the Pope was a right fella.

And then there was old Albert Young who had said 'Right' when asked to answer to the charge in court that he had killed a man in a fight at the Pikestone, 'Right, Your Honour', and got seven years for manslaughter. Now he sat in the sun outside his door, looking as gentle as anything, yet not to be trifled with or annoyed because of his past, but scurried past in case the stick his chin was leaning on was the same ashplant that had felled the man in the fight. Daddy said it had really been an accident and Albert was a quiet man unless he was roused, so no point in rousing him. The wall of the new gaol towered above Bridge Street, twenty feet high at this point because the County Surveyor's steamrollers and tar-boilers slept behind it. A lovely little blue flower grew in the cracks of the wall; Mr Smith said it grew on lime mortar and the only places it was found in Ireland were here and Cork, where he came from. He said it was called *Erinus alpinus*.

Artie Pollock said that the old name for Bridge Street was Friars' Lane because there had been a Franciscan monastery there, and that one of the gates – the Nun's Gate – in the Norman town wall had been built here. Bridge Street had been the main road to the Quoile Bridge before Church Street was built in 1837. Then came Mr Green's little chapel on the left, with a stone over the door saying that it had been built by Conway Pilson. Then there was Mrs Crawford's wall at Rathdune, a big house for a very cross lady who was always fighting with everybody. She would kick up a row if you as much as touched one of the bushes that hung out over the wall.

FIVE

IN 1938 BLACKMEN'S DAY WAS HELD IN
Downpatrick. The Blackmen, the Royal Black
Preceptory, were connected to the Orange Order,
which had an Orange Hall in Church Street with a
coloured arch across the road outside it every Twelfth
of July. The Blackmen did not hold their parade on
the Twelfth but on the last Saturday in August. Or,
to be more correct, they marched in August as well as
in July and several other times during the marching
season. This did not impinge much on Downpatrick
except when country lodges like Ballyclander or
Hollymount marched through on their way to the
Twelfth assembly somewhere, or the 'field', as they
called it. Often on a June evening you could hear the
music from the Inch or the outlying townlands as the
bands practised. Each year a different town in the
county was chosen as the venue for the Blackmen's
field: Blackmen from all over Down would converge
in groups to march through the streets out to a field
where there was a platform and speeches and then back

again. Now it was Downpatrick's turn, and most of them came in by train and the march was from the station up Market Street and out Church Street to a field at Finnebrogue just over the Quoile Bridge. They didn't go up Irish Street because the people in Irish Street generally did not like Orangemen marching there, much less John Street or Mary's Lane, but there was very little opposition to the march and generally the townspeople ignored them. There was no point in parading up English Street anyhow except to get to the cathedral and the only people who did that were the ex-servicemen of the British Legion, who marched to the war memorial on Remembrance Sunday, and groups like the Life Boys and the Boys' Brigade, who marched to one or other of the Protestant churches for church services.

The great Catholic parade was the children's excursion to Newcastle, known as the Canon's Excursion, held early in July each year, when all the children in the nuns' and Brothers' schools went on a day trip to Newcastle. This was entirely free and they got the train trip and a sandwich lunch and tea in Newcastle and the trip back. It was sometimes called the Catholic Twelfth because there were bands and banners and a march down through the town. Men collected money from the shopkeepers to pay for it. The children assembled about nine o'clock in the morning in the Brothers' school in Edward Street and marched down, class by class, led by the Catholic members of the council and the Canon in his car, with bands from Belfast and Newry playing hymns and Irish tunes and all the children in their classes with stewards and ushers and minders and helpers and, with the younger children, mothers and older sisters too, waving little papal flags and shouting, 'Three cheers for the Canon, hip, hip, hooray.' And being watched by great crowds of people along Irish Street and Market Street. The children were loaded into trains until they were all gone, perhaps a thousand of them, the town quiet and deserted until they returned. In Newcastle they repeated the process, marching up the town and back down to the Gaelic field for tea and sandwiches and games and ice cream and lemonade and sweets, and then marching up the town again and back to the station for the journey home.

In Downpatrick the town started to come to life again at about half past seven as people began to line the streets once more to see the children come home. There was less order this time, the Canon still in his Pied Piper role but the children were very tired and the parade swelled by some youths and older people who had gone over on the afternoon train (sixpence return on a Thursday); children carried coloured hats bought at the seaside and gaudy parasols and sticks of rock, some slept in their mothers' arms, but still there was the relentless tramp up the hill to Edward Street and dispersal, and cries of 'Three cheers for the Canon', but weaker now, though the Canon himself seemed rejuvenated by the day, face beaming in the sun under a big panama hat, saluting the crowds, proud of the children and how well turned out they were, proud of the parish, proud to show that they too could do it, could indeed do it better than Protestants, who didn't have the numbers in any case.

We never went on the excursion and never had any great desire to go jumping up and down the street in a parade and anyhow Newcastle was nothing special when you could go for threepence return any day in the summer. The excursion was probably a hangover from the time when many children did not get a holiday at all and a day at the seaside was a big treat. Daddy thought it was mad that Downpatrick shopkeepers had to pay in order to have all the money that families had saved spent on sweets and trinkets in shops in Newcastle. He was worried, too, by the effect on the water supply when Samson's Stone reservoir was emptied in the night as every child in the town had a bath and was scrubbed up for the parade. Mammy thought it was just using children to put on a display so that the Canon, who had been parish priest of Newcastle, could show off to his old parishioners that he was now in a better and bigger parish with more children and bigger schools.

One year, old Mrs Hanlon challenged me in the middle of the day when I went in to her vegetable shop for a message why I was not away on the excursion and said it was snobbish not to go. Mammy was cross and said that was the last cabbage she would buy from her but after a day or two she bought them again because Hanlons' vegetables were freshest and she could not do without them. I was glad because Hanlons' was easy to slip down to, on the other side of Market Street: out through the back gate, down the steps and along the narrow passage between the cinema and the chemist's shop which Ray called the narrow gauge. It was better organised than Tack Bell's or some of the other vegetable shops which were much smaller and did not have the same variety.

But back to the Blackmen. Mammy was delighted

when the march was fixed for Downpatrick because it was good for business and every room in the hotel would be occupied by one or other lodge needing lunches or meat teas or both, and we scrubbed out and opened up the old billiard room at the back and whitewashed some of the lofts in the yard and borrowed trestle tables from the Canon's Hall and the Masonic Hall and chairs and forms and benches from wherever to cater for the crowds. On the day, there were two or three sittings in some of the rooms as latecomers had to be fitted in. I set myself up a stall at the hall door to sell cigarettes, but nobody bought any and I quickly reverted to being a furniture remover and a clearer of tables and a runner for messages as we ran out of bread and milk and cooked ham and supplies had to be replenished.

Meantime, outside it was lodge after lodge, each with its own band, mostly flute bands with a thin reedy note, some accordion bands, and some rising to the splendour of a silver band. But the most persistent musical note was the throbbing of drums and the sound of feet marching. The men all wore black bowler hats and little coloured collarettes, each group led by a man with a more splendid sash than the others, and some of the men in front with a sword and a scabbard at the hip. And in front of each group were two men with pikestaffs, guarding the banner which flapped in the wind, held down ineffectually by two little boys hanging on to ribbons which were torn out of their hands as the banners bellied up nearly horizontal in the wind, the ribbons having to be retrieved again as the tail of the banner went sailing in the gale.

The banners were huge affairs, richly ornate, borne

by men on two poles, with a picture of King William on a horse, or Derry's walls, or Queen Victoria sitting on a throne surrounded by black children, or a Bible with written under it 'The secret of England's greatness'. There was a sprightly air as the men marched out to the field, but they were tireder and more limping as they came back in the late afternoon, at which time my forays to McGradys' for extra provisions became more often necessary. The stream of lodges was endless, with all traffic stopped and no way of getting across the road except by taking your life in your hands when there was a wider gap than usual between bands and running the gauntlet of the men with the pikes who didn't like people breaking up the procession, and then up the hill, impatient while Mr McGrady sliced the ham carefully and methodically, asking for judgements about thickness of slice and opinions about what was going on down the town, which he did not much care for, while all I could think about were customers who might walk out if they were not fed, or who would give the place a bad name. It was better when Jacky Moore was there. He just thumped the ham on to the slicer and turned the handle and let it rip until the pile looked just about the right weight — which it always was. Or Mrs McGrady, always good for a prayer and a gypsy cake and 'How's the Little Flower?' which was what she called Helen who was hard at work back at the hotel, washing dishes at the sink. Then down the hill at full speed, and running the gauntlet once again of the marching pikemen and the rain which had begun to fall while they were at the field.

The rain too was good for business. Although it

made the whole place messy and mats and bags had to be laid in the hall for people to wipe their feet and there were piles of dripping raincoats and umbrellas everywhere, it helped the bar trade. The hall and stairs were piled with drums and bits of equipment. There were bowler hats everywhere, each indistinguishable from the next. I wondered how the owners ever told them apart.

Late in the evening, frighteningly, the room suddenly darkened: somebody had set a banner against the windows. The room was like a cave. Then another banner was set against the wall outside, and another, until the front of the hotel was like a hall of tapestries, even in the rain. Somebody said there had been a row down the street because a publican called Rooney had told them to take their bloody banners to hell away from his front and there had been threats to burn him out. Auntie Lil said he was from Mourne as if that explained everything. Mammy said they were customers and as long as they paid the bills and behaved themselves and were spending money, they could put the twelve apostles and Moses and all the prophets and every king of England back to William the Conqueror against the wall and leave them there for all she cared.

Later in the same year there was an inter-county Gaelic match in Joe Smith's field at Monabot, out beyond Saul Camp where the South Down Militia used to train. Down were to play Cavan who were then one of the great teams while Down scarcely ever won a match. It was a big game to be played in an open field along the roadside where Joe Smith's cows grazed most of the time, a rocky, bumpy piece of ground above the level of the road with goal posts put up for the occasion and the pitch marked out with a whitewash brush and a bucket of lime and no nets or stands and no means of keeping the crowds back. There were no dressing rooms either, although the Down team got changed in one of the byres. The Cavan team stripped in the hotel where they had a meal before the game.

It was a horribly wet day and Daddy came in after mass to say that the match might not go on because the goal posts had been cut down in the night by Orangemen who objected to Sunday football and were trying to stop it, and Willie Byrne was very cross and wanted to catch somebody for it. Messages kept coming in that Cavan were on their way, that the game might be delayed but a crowd of bigots would not stop it, and that the goal posts had not been completely cut down because Joe Smith had heard the noise and come out in his night-shirt with a shotgun and chased the Orangemen off. Somehow new posts were got and put up or the others were repaired and new corner flags were put in place and the game went ahead. Down was beaten, easily enough in the end, although they played well for a time, Daddy said. Somehow nobody was ever caught, although everybody knew who had done it – three or four Protestant men, some of whom came into the bar regularly, but nobody ever mentioned it to them and they didn't brag about it. The only thing was that the next time there was a mission tent in the field next to the cricket ground it was knocked down one night, but whether there was any connection, I don't know. Some people said it was the wind that blew it down and there must have been a sudden squall because nobody in the town, and no Catholic, would do that sort of thing. Mammy said it was a queer squall that carried a cross-cut saw in its tool kit.

Police were not very popular and were generally not trusted. There were of course people like Sergeant Lowry, who let us play handball in the alley behind the barracks, and old Tommy Donaldson and Joe Russell who had been in the town for years and whom everybody liked because they never arrested anybody and never had a case. The ones to watch were those who came looking for promotion and who would be out checking the pubs after hours or lightless bicycles. I remember Mr Johnston one night seeing a man talking to an unpopular sergeant who was sitting on the sofa in the bar. Afterwards, Johnson warned the man, 'Mind what you say to that fellow. Anything you say will be taken down and altered and used in evidence against you.' Another grumpy Protestant shopkeeper, hearing a policeman boast that he was the youngest to have attained his rank, snarled, 'You must have done something dirty for that.'

Generally, though, married policemen lived around the town and their children went to the schools and were very much part of the community. The tone was set by each head constable, who could take a hard line or an easy one. There were a couple of Kerrymen in succession whom Daddy knew and they were fairly easy-going. One particular martinet was known as Tail-light because his speciality was chasing people who had bad brakes or no tail-lights on their bicycles and bringing them to court where they would be fined a shilling. He went round the town on a Satur-day night with a blackthorn stick, keeping order among the drunks and clearing out the pubs at nine o'clock. His bark was more fierce than his bite and he would argue and bally-rag and maybe thump people or poke them with his stick, but without doing any more about it. One chronic drunk called Jimmy had been fed such a diet of westerns in the pictures, Roy Rogers, Tom Mix, Gene Autry, Hopalong Cassidy, that when he had had enough tony wine or other cheap drink he relapsed into a sort of cowboy lingo. When Tail-light threatened to put him in the barracks for the night, Jimmy would drawl, 'Gee, Sheriff, you don't think I'm afraid of your little calaboose?' And when asked for his address he would say airily, 'Buenos Aires, in the Argentine. You'll find it on a meat tin any day.'

Whatever about the police, the B Specials were despised and distrusted. Most of them were known as people of not much class who had been given a uniform and a gun and a licence to stop and harass people they did not like. The people who liked them least were the regular policemen who thought they gave policing a bad name and gave them a wide berth. The B Specials particularly annoyed people whom they knew well by stopping them and asking for their names, and often, if they were young people, making nasty, provocative remarks to see if their victims would try to hit them, in which case they were in real trouble. People were afraid, too, because in the country lanes you might easily find you were on your own and there were no witnesses.

SIX

INSIDE THE WINDOW OF THEIR SHOP AT THE bottom of Market Street, Mr Waterman the shoe-maker sat with his sons Harry and Isadore. The workbench was placed across the window looking out on the street to give the maximum amount of light on the work. They did not like to be called cobblers like the other shoemakers and repairers on the street, but makers of fine shoes. They also did repairs. On the workbench were three slots into which the shanks of the lasts could be shoved; the lasts were of many differ-ent sizes to allow for different shapes and sizes of shoes. The shoemakers all wore white aprons down over the lap and covering the knees and with a wide pouch across the belly like a kangaroo's for holding hammers and knives. They sat cross-legged on a board platform in the window, their knees splayed under the bench, although sometimes they would slide back on their backsides so as to handle the work on their laps. The hollow in the apron between the thighs and down into the crotch often filled with bits of leather pared off the sides of soles and had to be shaken off with the hands when they stood up to stretch their legs.

On a sloping ledge at the bottom of the window, just inside the glass, were examples of their workmanship: shoes handsewn and carefully tooled with the welts evenly milled and the lace eyelets perfectly aligned, and the toecaps tooled and the heels decorated. The shoes were of fine leather, highly polished, and they were displayed in pairs, one shoe showing the upper and the other the brightly burnished sole. There were certificates too in neat black lettering and Gothic script, framed in narrow black frames, stating that the shoes had been awarded a diploma at some exhibition and had been highly commended by the Guild of Master Shoemakers. Apparently the patron saint of shoemakers was Saint Crispin and Saint Crispin's Day was the date of the battle of Agincourt, so at the bottom of each framed certificate there was a quotation from Shakespeare's *Henry V*:

> This day is called the feast of Crispian.
> He that outlives this day, and comes safe home,
> Will stand a tip-toe when this day is nam'd,
> And rouse him at the name of Crispian.
> . . .
> And Crispin Crispian shall ne'er go by,
> From this day to the ending of the world,
> But we in it shall be remembered;
> We few, we happy few, we band of brothers.

Further up the street the shoemakers put boxes of factory shoes in the window, like McCartans', or, like Cassidys', hung a large side of leather on the wall with prices written on it in white chalk.

The Watermans were very proud of their work-manship and of their making of hand-stitched shoes. You could watch old Mr Waterman with an awl in his fist, driving it through the double thickness of leather in the sole and the welt, the palm of his hands protected by a sort of leather half-mitten with no fin-gers. He would press down with the ball of his hand on the top of the wooden handle to drive the pointed spike through, and pull it out again, easing it a bit in a circular movement to get the blade free and ready to pierce the next hole. He would take the long wax-end, twist the point between his finger and thumb, and thread it through the hole. He would pull it tight and centre it so that the ends were even and he would thread one end from the top and the other from the bottom through the next hole, cross them in a knot, and pull them up. The last tightening was done by wrapping one end of the waxed cord round the handle of the awl in his right hand and looping the other round his left hand, protected by its leather mitt, and pulling as tight as could be. Then on to another hole bored, another cord threaded, another knot pulled tight, painstakingly round the welt of the shoe until it was all neatly stitched.

Meantime at the next last Harry was soling and heeling a pair of shoes, cutting the shape out of a side of leather that had been steeped overnight to make it workable. The form of the sole was cut out by placing a sharp metal shape on top of the leather and hammer-ing it down. Then it was flexed in the hand to make it pliable and placed on top of the shoe on the last and held in place with one tack in the middle, then shaped a bit more at the edges with a sharp knife, little slices being cut off to make the sole fit the size of the welt, and a scrape being made with the point of a knife, held down the blade, with the forefinger against the side of the welt and run quickly round to provide a line to guide the placement of nails. Next, the sole was fixed with nails put in at regular intervals, a handful scooped up from the open bag and held in the mouth, then taken three or four at a time into the palm of the left hand, fed out singly between the thumb and forefinger and placed point down against the leather in the groove; a tap with the narrow end of the hammer, then a twist and three taps with the heavy end, and the nail would be beaten down with a rat-tat-tat, quicker almost than the eye could see, until a line of bright brass sparables marched round the edge making a continuous beading along the rim. Harry would make a few strokes of the knife to clean off the edge, and a few slices at the end of the sole near the instep, and beat in another line of nails straight across the bottom of the sole, and the shoe would be handed to Izzy to finish off and polish on the buffing wheel worked by a treadle at the side. Izzy also made the wax-ends out of lengths of cotton twine or linen thread three or four feet long, cut off the spool and laid together and lightly twisted and then drawn through a ball of beeswax held in the hollow of the left hand, and pulled out as far as the arm could reach until they were well impregnated with wax, then rolled with the palm of the hand against the top of the thigh until they formed a twisted, even waxed cord, the two ends now being taken and waxed again until they were stiff points, almost like a needle, ready to be pushed through the smallest pinhole.

The Watermans did not work on a Saturday and the shop did not open, you saw just the gaping windows and nobody at the bench, the lasts standing bare, but the framed certificates and the prize-winning shoes proudly displayed at the bottom. This was because they were Jews and Saturday was their Sunday, the Sabbath, the seventh day on which the Lord rested. Joan said they cooked all their meals on Friday for the weekend and did not have a fire on the Sabbath, or cook, but just said prayers instead. The shop did not open on a Sunday either because all the others were closed too; we thought the Jews were very lucky, or very clever, to have two holidays. Once, after Mrs Waterman died, the boys did not shave for weeks, and even Izzy who was usually chubby-faced grew a straggly sort of beard. Ray said that was the Jewish way of mourning and it went on for a long time and showed how much they respected their mother. They had ceremonies such as Passover when they went to the synagogue in Belfast. Daddy was very friendly with Mr Waterman whom he met to chat with on a Sunday when we took a walk out the Ballydugan Road towards the racecourse. He said his real name was Wassermann and he had come to Downpatrick before the Great War from the Ukraine in Russia where he had been very badly treated, and he was a fine craftsman and a very religious man and it was a lesson to everybody not to be afraid of people because they were different.

Daddy said he did not like putting people in separate boxes because of their religion or colour or politics. He thought they were all the same – one lot as bad as the other, all pretty hopeless when it came to the bit, and inclined to fight and squabble about things that did not matter at all like flags and favours and slogans and songs. Mammy thought so too. She told a story about Daniel O'Connell in Kerry being hailed by a man mending holes in the road who told him to win his case and pull down the landlords. O'Connell replied, 'I will be back this way tomorrow, and whether I win or lose, you will still be breaking stones.'

Mammy was very much against class distinction and agreed with Auntie Lil that the colonel's lady and Julia O'Grady were sisters under the skin. I wondered whether this was any friend of the McGradys in Market Street, but I decided probably not. Mammy's favourite text from the Gospels was 'In my Father's house there are many mansions'. She believed that there was room for all in Heaven, that most people who half tried would get there, and that God would be merciful rather than stern at the end. She was very charitable and contributed endlessly in small amounts to the missions and black babies and poor Chinamen and priests and nuns who wrote to her to build churches and chapels in poor parts of cities in England, and sometimes even cathedrals. In business she was more suspicious. One of her maxims was 'Call everyone a thief and you'll never be done'. At the same time she was very conscious of the duty to love her neighbour, as she said, quoting the old Penny Catechism: 'Mankind of every description'. She used to console herself by saying that that didn't mean you had to like them. Indeed the less you liked, the more merit there was in the love.

SEVEN

THE STATION WAS ANOTHER PLACE OF wonder, with the trains coming in every couple of hours, and sometimes oftener, from Belfast, Newcastle, Ardglass and Killough. Then it was a hive of activity. At other times it was quiet enough and good to ramble around, so long as you kept out of the way of Mr Foster the stationmaster who did not like little boys lurking around his station. Mr Sam Pyper, who lived up English Street with his daughter, was a big man in the railway and he walked down the street every morning to get the train. A portly florid man, he usually stepped very sedately and saluted my mother as he passed. She said he had a special compartment to himself on the train to Belfast. Nobody travelled first-class except Mr Pyper. Black coat, striped trousers, winged collar, watch chain, frock coat, corporation, his protruding stomach causing him to teeter downhill, into Johnnie Moore's for the news-paper. He never used the short cut through the yard – needn't rush – they would wait for him anyhow.

The best thing to do at the station was to pretend that you were waiting for a parcel. You could go to Jim Cochrane in the parcels office and ask and he would go through his lists and turn over boxes on the ground to see if it was there and poke around in shelves to make sure and say it must be on the next train. If it was not too long to wait you could go in to the fire in the waiting room, if it was a cold day (but not the first-class waiting room, nobody went there, not even Mr Pyper), or sit on the seats on the platform, or go down to look at the books in the window of Eason's bookstall. This was a wooden kiosk built against the back wall of the platform like an overgrown telephone box, painted brown to simulate grained oak and with books displayed inside the windowpanes. The front was closed by a rolling shutter which rolled up to disclose a counter on which the morning papers were arranged neatly, and racks on the back with magazines and a few paperback books. These were mostly detective stories by Sexton Blake or westerns by Zane Grey. There were also soppy books for girls by Ethel M. Dell. My mother called them 'penny dreadfuls', but they always seemed to cost threepence or fourpence. The kiosk also displayed, when the front was open, the friendly face and the top half of the body of Cissie McCabe, who opened it in time for the trains in the morning, closed it in the afternoon, and sometimes kept a lonely vigil in the evenings, after the *Tele*, the *Belfast Telegraph*, arrived in when there were very few customers. I think she was glad of the company because she would let you read the papers without paying for them provided you sat quietly on the seat and folded them up very carefully when you had finished. Cissie was very decent and she would let you have a good look at a book before you bought it. Sometimes you could read a whole book in this way in three or four goes. Somehow paperbacks were thought to be a bit wicked, not really respectable books like hardbacks, but then these were more expensive: if you didn't manage to borrow them from the library, they could cost a shilling, or even half a crown.

Round behind the bookstall, behind a high wall at the other platform, where the rails stopped just short of buffers built into the wall, was a doorway marked GENTS. This was an opening rather than a door: there was no door or flap or gate on it. It led to a urinal, whitewashed and smelling strongly of a mixture of lime, chlorine, carbolic, ammonia and above all, urine. You were not really supposed to go there, no matter how short-taken, because it was a dirty place and the Lord knew what disease you might catch, and God only knew who you would meet there.

Who we were most likely to meet there, if not in the toilet then lurking outside, was an exact little man, not any taller than we were and very finely made, called Mr Emerick. Mr Emerick was nattily dressed and wore a bright yellow waistcoat: the waistcoat heightened the impression of some small, exotic, gaily plumed cage bird. Mr Emerick was an inmate in the County Lunatic Asylum who had been there for years and who was allowed to wander around the town in his lucid moments. He told us wonderful stories about his travels around the world, speaking in a clipped, precise English accent that we thought very grand. If it happened today, Mr Emerick would be put in gaol and we young boys might be taken into care, but I cannot recall any improper word or gesture, or any reason to fear the bird man, or to have anything but affection for him. What we did fear, and what gave the whole thing a spice of conspiracy and danger, was Daddy coming off the train and finding us hanging round the station, although if you were quick enough you could pretend that you had come down to meet him.

Mr Emerick had a gold watch on a chain hanging across his chest. He would take the watch out of his fob pocket, flick the cover open with his thumbnail, and say, 'Do you see this watch, boys? I got it as a reward for an act of bravery, for diving, fully dressed, off Sydney Harbour Bridge in Australia in order to save a man from drowning.' Since Sydney Harbour Bridge was one of the wonders of the modern world illustrated in the volumes of *Wonderland of Knowledge* that Daddy had got by sending away coupons in the *Daily Mail*, we quickly recognised Mr Emerick's action as heroism indeed, a claim to fame that left us gasping. Years later I found myself in a boat passing under Sydney Harbour Bridge and looked up at the lattice of ironwork and the awesome drop to the choppy waters. Another idol tumbled, another article of faith denied, I had to confess, 'Mr Emerick, I don't believe you did.'

Market Street was the hub of the town. The only big houses, apart from the banks, were those opposite the railway station; they had been built to cash in on the trade the trains were expected to bring. Daddy said that the railway, which had been a boon to most other towns, had drained the life out of Downpatrick because it made it easier for people to do business in Belfast. Now that the buses were competing with the railway, with a green bus sitting outside the station ready to start at the same time as the train, and to go there direct and faster, and to bring people right into the centre of Belfast, it would be no time at all until the railway went bankrupt and the trains stopped running.

Market Street was lively, day and night, because there were shops and stores and pubs there and because there were dozens of children living in the street. The bank managers lived over the banks (except the Ulster, whose manager had a big house on the Circular Road), the shopkeepers lived over their shops, the station-master dwelled in the station and the gas manager in the gas house. Market Street was defined by the Fair Green and the Market House and Yard at one end, and by the *Down Recorder* office at the other. There were two blacksmiths' forges and a bicycle shop which was gradually turning itself into a garage for cars with a petrol pump mounted on the footpath outside. There was a cinema which attracted great crowds every night, and especially on Saturday and Sunday.

In off the street, through large arched gateways, were all sorts of workshops. Harry Blaney, who had played billiards with Daddy in Killough, upholstered furniture in the workshop behind his new furniture store, the door open wide to give light, hammering, cutting, tacking, the nails held in his mouth and fed out with the tongue to a little hammer with a magnet on the end touched against the lips. He had brought the hammer back from America with him and all the time as he worked he managed to talk to Daddy with a strong American accent. There was Willie Denvir, the locksmith, who could turn his hand to anything, and Bertie Brown's brother Bob who fixed farm machinery. On the other side, behind the Belfast Bank, in Mosey Porter's yard the auctions were held every week. They were full of furniture and old carpets and rolls of linoleum stacked against the wall and old farm implements waiting to be sold. Like the hotel yard, Mr Porter's yard was a short cut from Market Street to English Street. Once during an auction an old lady shouted up to Mosey that there were holes in the roll of lino he was selling. He shouted back very rudely, telling her where there were holes in her too. On Market Street too were bookies' shops, which were supposed to be illegal but which were the busiest of the lot, entered through harmless sweetie shops or down back alleys or through doors set into the wall with no sign or marking.

At Breens' corner, the junction with Irish Street, the street sloped steeply from the crown of the road to the footpath. Buses trying to get round the right-angled bend often came over the kerb, threatening your toes if you were standing there, or tilted so much that you thought they were going to slide into the corner shop.

Mammy was always very particular that we should salute clergymen of every denomination, and nuns and Brothers too. They were people who had dedicated themselves to God, she said, and the cloth they wore deserved respect. Every Roman collar was a signal for caps to be doffed and forelocks touched and for a courteous greeting and reply. Now the Dean of Down was a very bad driver with a very long car who always had trouble getting round Breens' corner without crossing the white line or sliding into the kerb. It was always a particular thrill to see him coming and to wait at the point of the corner to salute him. He, for his part, was so pleased when little Catholic boys lifted their red school caps to salute him that he would lift his hands off the steering wheel to salute us in return. This invariably caused the car to lurch wildly into the footpath as the camber of the road caught the front wheels, and we wondered if it would actually plough through the shop window. The only thing that would have increased the pleasure was if the Canon, who was an even worse driver, although his problem was speed, had come in the opposite direction at the same time and crashed into the Dean.

The other thrill was to see a large, high car drive up Market Street with apparently no driver at all. When it got close you saw the brim of a lady's hat peeping up just above the steering wheel. This was little Miss Forde of Seaforde in to do her shopping.

Just across the road from the corner was an entry leading into even greater delights: the printing works of the *Down Recorder* and Chambers's paintshop where they mixed the paints. There was also the County Club, behind an anonymous front door, where Mr Johnston the solicitor did his drinking on Sundays. The police did not raid the County Club because the County Inspector and the District Inspector drank there too.

The printshop had huge machines on the ground floor, with great rollers with ink in them, into which the paper was fed by hand, sheet by sheet. The wet roller came across to coat the type with ink in its bed, then a sheet of paper was flicked over by a projecting arm, and another roller came over to make the impression. The sheet of paper had to be snatched away again before the inked roller came back and the cycle started again. It was all rollers and ratchets and long canvas bands like in a threshing machine which would draw you in and crush you, or take off a leg or a hand if you went too near.

Upstairs in a rickety loft were the compositors, the typesetters, standing in front of tilted wooden boxes divided up with a separate little compartment for each letter of the alphabet. The small letters were at the bottom and the capitals at the top. The written text was stuck on a spike at the top of the box while they picked the metal letters individually out of the box with tweezers and set them in a frame held in the left hand, letter by letter, word by word, line by line, with blank metal pieces put in to make the spaces. They had to put the type together back to front so that it would come out right when printed. They worked at great speed. When a block of type was finished it was put into a frame, with metal strips to mark the lines between the vertical columns, and locked in place on the bed of the printing press. The paper came out on a Saturday about six o'clock in the morning to be in time to catch the bread carts before they started off on their country rounds; the compositors worked all week, but particularly on a Friday night to get it out.

Old Mr Crichton ran the paper. He was very keen on cricket and had played too. Daddy told me about a man called Johnny Morgan who had objected to something that had been printed about him in the paper. Next week there was a note saying that it had been a typographical error. Shortly after that, Mr Crichton was playing cricket and was bowled out first ball. Johnny Morgan was standing watching over the hedge on the Strangford Road, and he roared with glee: 'A batographical error!'

Chambers's paint shop was on the other side of the entry. Alfie Oakes mixed paint for the men to take out on jobs and talked about football to anybody who would listen. It was all there, red lead, white lead, raw oil, boiled oil, linseed and turps, thinners and driers, yellow ochre, umber, burnt sienna, carmine, Prussian blue, and the colours blending in the pot as it was stirred, and being tried out in the light for shade and tone, brushed on to the back of the door or the plastered wall which looked like some mad mosaic of colour. A painter from Portaferry who had a lovely singing voice gave me a book called *The Ragged Trousered Philanthropists* which he said was the painter's bible. It didn't seem very religious to me. And in the corner, glass was being cut into panes on a bench covered with green baize. Mr Chambers was painting a signboard, blocking out the letters in chalk, filling in the shapes and adding squiggles and flourishes, rubbing in gold leaf from a little booklet, the pages separated by tissue paper. And men all around were talking about their trade, about burning off and sanding and pumice and washing down, and about scumbling and mottling and stippling and stencilling and varnishing and graining, and the work of old tradesmen long dead which could be recognised at a glance. Nobody like them now.

EIGHT

ALL THE TIME THE TALK WAS OF THE CIVIL war in Spain, not only in the newspapers but at school and in church. Auntie Lil remembered the horrors of the civil war in Kerry and said civil war was the worst possible sort of war. The sermons were about the awful godless communists who were persecuting the Church like the penal days in Ireland, and mass rocks and priests on the run and Catholics not able to own a horse worth more than five pounds. Priests and nuns, they said, were taken in Spain and crucified or shot in the churches or cut up on the very altars, and people were locked into churches where they had taken refuge and the buildings were torched, and sacrilege and desecration occurred everywhere. There were prayers for Franco and General O'Duffy who was supposed to be bringing an army of blueshirts to fight the reds. In Alfie Oakes's paint pot, red and blue made purple and I wondered what would happen when the colours met in Spain. It was war all right, but far away, and not, in

Daddy's phrase, 'immediate and terrible war'.

The Munich bother registered with us because Mammy's recollection of the Great War frightened her, and in particular the years of separation that had meant from her new husband, and the number of husbands and sons who did not return. And Auntie Lil had lost her husband of a few days to a ship called the *Laurentic* mined in Lough Swilly and a lonely grave in Buncrana. This had made both sisters confirmed pacifists, and my father was not a warmonger either. So we had additional prayers for peace or for the avoidance of war added to the rosary every night.

The newspapers were full of the Sudetenland and maps of Central Europe with Austria and part of Germany shaded to look like a wolf's head with Czechoslovakia caught in the jaws, about to be swallowed up and devoured. Then came the anxious wait by the wireless, the old black Philco brought from Killough and placed above a gun case in the sitting room, with wires trailing under the linoleum across to the window to the earth terminal and the outside aerial. There, amid the spluttering and the static, we heard Mr Chamberlain promise peace in our time. And we thought of the Czechs as a faraway people, not much to do with us, and we all flopped down on our knees for a rosary of thanksgiving and Mammy cried because Daddy would not be taken away and Ray would not be conscripted and sent to the front as cannon fodder for the generals. Daddy said now they would soon sort out the Spanish thing and I heard someone else say that Hitler would probably sort out the border in Ireland too.

I won praise in a class debate at school for a stirring

representation of Hitler and a contemptuous put-down of Chamberlain, the little man with the rolled umbrella, a Chaplin figure crawling to Berchtesgaden to sue for peace. Even the arrival of the Utitzes from Czechoslovakia to stay at the hotel did not alert us to anything more sinister. The Utitzes came with a mountain of luggage and occupied the whole top floor of the hotel for weeks while they tried to start a factory in Killyleagh and looked for a house for themselves. There was old grandfather Doctor Jacob, a distinguished-looking man with a silver goatee beard and a black coat who looked as if he might have stepped out of one of the Dutch paintings reproduced on the walls in school. He spoke no English, but hummed the tune of an English popular song of the time. There were also the younger Mr and Mrs Utitz and a boy of about my own age called Eric who also spoke no English. They had brought with them the process and the patent for a special sort of leather called UTA chrome and they were going to take over the old spinning mill and turn it into a tannery. We thought of them only as rich people who were getting out with their money, but Daddy said they would be a great boon to the area because they would give employment in their factory.

There was the threat of war, but there was fishing too, which meant a trip to the Roughal, a far cry from the rowing boats and the surging seas off Killough, where you hauled fish out by the bagful, or even the excitement of taking mackerel off the rocks; fishing the Roughal was sedate, sitting on a river bank all day waiting for the fish to bite, but satisfying and rewarding in its own way. First there were the preparations. Down to Dicksons' for a pole and line. The poles were kept in a lower store, down a long passageway lined with assorted ironmongery and hundreds of little wooden drawers, each with a yellow label on it saying what length of screws it held, and whether flat-headed, round-headed, or pointed or with male or female thread, and boxes of bolts and nuts with samples tied with twine on the outside, and piles of binder twine and heaps of baling wire and long-tailed shovels leaning against the wall and garden spades for digging, and graips and pitchforks and navvies' shovels, down, down, down away from the light of the shop and into the dimness of the store with the only light coming in from a half-opened gate out into Market Street. Here, where there was headroom, the bamboo poles could be held up in the air and tested for length and strength and stability and swishiness. Then back up to the brightness of the shop where old Hans Hayes with his white moustache presided behind the counter which had a long strip of brass screwed to its back edge and marked out in feet and inches. And you had to inspect several thicknesses of snouden, a hard cord used for fishing lines, before a choice could be made – would it be too light to hold the fish we hoped to catch, or so heavy as to make a splash and frighten them all away? And how long should it be, without a reel, just to be thrown out and hauled in again? And there was a hook to be selected, and a piece of catgut so that the line would be invisible in water and the fish would not see the bit attached to the worm which hid the hook. And little screw-in round eyes to form a track along the rod for the line and to keep it tidy. Then up to the yard to assemble it all, with good knots learned from the real fishermen in Killough and not silly grannies which would slip out the first time a fish put them to the test, and a sinker made of lead gas pipe, carefully beaten out flat and wrapped round the line to bring it down, and a cork from the box under the cork-drawer in the bar, selected carefully and tied on to keep it up, and some worms dug out of Mammy's flowerbed and carried, wriggling and writhing, red and brown, in a glass jam jar with a piece of string tied round the lip for a carrier, and flat slaters found under slabs in the yard or in damp corners of stables, creeping and crawling, crammed into an old tobacco tin to provide an alternative bait if the fish did not like the worms. And sometimes Mammy made me a sandwich which I put in my bag with a lemonade bottle full of milk, so that I could spend the whole day at Roughal. 'There,' she would say. 'Off to the Waxies' Dargle.' But she never said what it meant, and I wondered if it meant anything.

Then off at a gallop up English Street, past Captain Sloane's with the wrought-iron lamp bracket on the corner of the railings, and the old cannon sunk in the footpath as a bollard, up Wallace's Lane to the great granite gateway of Down High School. In over the stone stile to the triangular field, which was easier than getting through the swinging iron gate, arranged like half a turnstile, difficult to squeeze through at the best of times, impossible if you were carrying a rod and line and all the other bits and pieces. Along the path under the towering bluestone wall of the gaol, with its massive granite coping stones, avoiding Fanny Breen's tethered and langled goats, looking for the barely visible start of the path that led down the steep bank and towards the Mount.

The Mount was a wonder, magical, a place of mystery that only the knowing could make their way into, a secret not to be shown to everybody but to be kept to ourselves, received in trust and shown only to close neighbours. But first to look out, standing on the drystone wall at the bottom of the bank, to see where Bohills' cows were, and particularly the bull, in the big field that stretched right to the edge of the marshes, across the drain and on again to be swallowed in the flatness of the river. And having sighted cattle, to decide whether one of them might be the bull, or young bullocks frisky for a chase, and to weigh up the chances of getting across to the Mount before being chased and gored and destroyed by the bull. Then having carefully concealed every bit of red fabric (no point in annoying the bull more than absolutely necessary), out under the barbed wire, screeching against rusty iron stakes set in the rickety stonework of the crumbling wall, and down a drop of a couple of feet into the field, the rod and gear laid on the grass inside while the wall is traversed, barbed wire held up with one hand to avoid a finger being snapped or a jersey torn or trousers ripped, then recovered, standing on the lower side and easing the length of the bamboo pole in between the iron stakes, watching out not to snag it on the strands and not to get the line tangled and not to catch the rod on the stakes or to drop the jar of worms or to spill the slaters.

Then down the hill at a gallop, using the slope to get up speed for the run up to the Mount, dodging the cow claps, jumping a big one and missing and plopping right down into the middle and squirting brown stinking sticky liquid up the calves of the legs and over the top of the foot. And weighing the danger of attack by cattle against the discomfort of shit and stopping to take off the sandal, smelling the rich putrefaction of the cow clap, pulling a wisp of grass and finding a docken leaf to wipe off the legs, rubbing the bare foot up and down in the grass, trying to get the dirt out from between the toes without cutting yourself on a sharp blade of grass, rubbing the sole of the sandals and cleaning off the strap and the inside with more grass plucked up in a handful and then thrown away.

The Mount is a great green fortress floating above the marshes: in the morning, mist on the low ground making it stick up like an island in a white sea, in winter surrounded by water and inaccessible, but most of the time just sitting there solid and impenetrable, no way in, no way through, blocking the route to the Roughal unless you are prepared to go round the outside, miles and miles in the fields, wet underfoot, crossed by drains which have to be jumped with all your load, and some too broad to do so with safety, and Minnie Martin's meadow and Protestant cows even more dangerous than Bohills' and Thompsons' bullocks, hungrier and fiercer. From the outside the Mount is a mass of growth, whins, alders, brambles, boortrees: solid, compact and symmetrical. There is a way through, for those who know, lightly marked in the grass by the feet of initiates, beaten too between the clumps of whins by the feet of cattle seeking shelter from the sun, and opening here and there into flat patches of beaten grass and bracken where beds have been made.

On inspection the Mount turns out not to be solid at all but a series of circumvallations of defensive ramparts thrown up and deep entrenchments, a fortification such as the Gauls might have erected to withstand Caesar, the work of human hands and not just of nature. The map says it is called Rathkeltair but Arthur Pollock says this is wrong and nobody in the town calls it anything but the Mount. Arthur says Celtair was a cross old Celtic chief who had his fort on the cathedral hill, and the Mount was built in a couple of days by a fierce old Norman knight called John de Courcy as a defence after he had captured the abbey and beaten the Irish.

This helped to make sense out of the place. When you got to the top of the first ridge there was a deep drop and a wide flat area, more a valley than a trench, from which another steep bank arose on the other side, and which you could imagine being full of water. The sides were overgrown so that you had to zig-zag between the bushes, down and up again. Then you crossed another rampart and another deeper trench before beginning the hazardous crawl up a low tunnel formed by overhanging branches crossed by angry barbed and springy brambles with thorns like razors, ready to gash and slash and tear, to slice the skin and snag the gansey and slit the trousers, hard to lift, then flying back into place, impossible to break, hard to trample down in sandals and bare legs, harder still to jump over with the overhanging alders, fortified by whins and bracken and finally secured by patches of slippery mud, which had to be crawled through on hands and knees, and lumps of cow dung of various degrees of consistency depending on when the cattle had last passed through and what sort of vegetation they had eaten before they had done so. And so it was, up and up, slowly like climbers on a mountain face, like spies infiltrating a fortress, like the Fianna passing through a wood without breaking a leaf above or crushing the grass below, and all the time in a cave formed of interlacing, interlocking branches and fronds through which the light fell in a lacework of rays and columnar sunbeams, leaving mysterious pools of semi-darkness, climbing into the face of the bank, steeper and steeper, and the sides of the track worn deeper and deeper into the soil, pulling the rod behind, pushing the other bits and pieces in front until finally the breakthrough, out into the glorious sunshine and a wide level expanse of green that looks like a lawn, with a path snaking across it to an almost hidden gap in the outside rampart where the escape hatch is located which leads to the downward path on the other side.

If you have time to wait, the top of the Mount is a large oval enclosure surrounded by a grass bank. It is a magic, lonely, private place with no noise but the birds, cut off from the world, lonely but not frightening. The ground is smooth, the grass short and the whole place full of rabbits. Towards the far end there is a small mound which turns out to be in the middle of another rampart, sticking up like a navel, from the top of which you can see over the outer ramparts to the cathedral and the river and the bottom end of the town and the top of Gallows Hill and over across the marshes to the woods of Hollymount and the backdrop of the Mourne peaks and Slieve Croob. The Mount's last summit is not easily achieved. The path is not so tortuous or so hidden as that up the outside, but it is not so well defined either, and the sides of the ditch are steep and the face of the mound is pocked with rabbit holes. Indeed the whole surface of the oval patch is criss-crossed with rabbit tracks and with runs and you would have to be careful not to put your foot into one of Hammy Young's snares, a running noose made out of fine thin wire and pegged to the ground at the side of the track just where it passes a tuffet of grass, or behind a small whin bush. But there is a large field with no snares, and this is great territory for running and jumping and having your own Olympic or tailteann games and for rolling your eggs at Easter. Daddy has a book that says that the people of the town used to have games and races here every Easter Tuesday and you could see that they would want to do that.

The mound in the inner ring was the centre of all, the tip-top, the citadel. Arthur said it was called a bailey and there would have been a wooden roundhouse on it. But it could be Custer's last stand, or the Alamo, or Tara, or Eamain Macha or Saint Patrick on Slemish or Gallipoli depending on what game you wanted to play. And the narrow path could be Thermopylae to be guarded by three hundred men, or Horatio's bridge over the Tiber to be secured by three, and the whole Mount could be Vercingetorix camp at Alesia, ready to withstand the Romans, or the Forbidden City, or the Heights of Abraham to be scaled in the dark.

But to get to the fishing, you had to follow the right path through the grass and spot exactly the right gap in the whins at the top of the outside rampart and creep under the branches and slither and slide down to the bottom again. Then up out of the ditch and round the shoulder of a hill on a path along the edge of the marshes and there, flat and grey and stretching away on both sides, was the Roughal. And there too would be a couple of boys who had come up from the lower end of the town along the loaning at the war memorial, and Mr Preston who had a reel on his rod and all sorts of lures who had come along the side of the drain at Minnie Martin's meadow at the bottom of Church Street.

You could look back and see that although you had seemed to come for miles by secret routes, and although it was a cut-off sort of place, you were really quite near the lower end of the town. You could see the low houses on Newbridge Street stretching along the roadway under Malone's Hill, and green and white buses passing in front of them, and Mrs Crawford's house at Rathdune in its gardens up on the hill behind, and on the other shore, dark and mysterious among the trees, the ruins of Inch Abbey. The vista was closed at one end where Kary Hill intersected with Portallo wood, appearing to make a lake of the river, and opening at the other across the flatness of the marshes to the backdrop of Slieve Croob.

The Roughal is part of the river Quoile. Indeed only a short stretch of it, but wide and lined with reeds and rushes and almost cut off at each end by a bend and a hill stretching out, and looking more like a lake than a river, and not flowing very fast at all, indeed mostly showing no perceptible movement, so unlike the tides at Killough. This is deceptive because the river here could gobble you up and devour you in a minute, and you were only allowed to go there to fish if you swore not to go into the water, not to take your shoes off, and certainly not to swim. This was necessary because the river claimed someone every seven years and Stanley Smith had been drowned there three or four years before (which seemed to leave the way clear for another three or four years, but apparently that was not the way the river did its sums). Here too the monks had been at their work. When they were chased out of Inch Abbey by the Maxwells who had taken over Finnebrogue, they threw all their sacred vessels and the bell of the abbey into the Roughal, where it would ring every seven years; then the river would claim its victim. And when the abbey was restored to the Catholics, as it surely would be one day, and mass was said there again, the bell would float back from the bottom of the river and up again into the belfry and ring incessantly with joy and this time there would be no talk of victims or drownings and all those who had perished would enter into heaven if they were not there already. And if past history was not enough to make the river a dangerous place to bathe in, there was supposed to be a tunnel under the riverbed which might collapse if you walked on top of it and drown you that way. There was said to be a ford across the river further down near Jane's Shore, but given all the warnings nobody was going to look for it, and those people who crossed over from one side to the other on the ice when the river was frozen in a very hard winter were known to be tempting fate and risking extinction by at least two different routes.

Most of this information was gathered from boys at school who had lived all their lives in the town. It was Catholic lore and not the sort of thing you discussed with Mr Preston, although it seemed mean not to let

him and the little Protestant boys know the real nature
of the dangers that lurked under the placid waters of
the Roughal. The hidden tunnel was a safe enough
topic, and the ford and the ice, and Mammy's warnings about holes in the riverbed and weeds along the
edge which could reach out and pull you in if you
were not careful.

The Quoile is a river of many names, and Mr Preston
knows them all. Down at the narrow bit, between the
floodgates and Jane's Shore, running underneath the
arches of the old stone bridge that carried the main road
to Belfast and Killyleagh, it is just the Quoile. Then it is
the Roughal, past Portallo wood and Inch Abbey and
round the bend to the pile bridge where the railway
line crosses over. Then it is the Rann, then the
Annacloy river, then the Kilmore river where it splits
into the Crossgar river and the Ballynahinch river; and
the Crossgar river goes on to become a trickle along
the roadside, a mere stream, the Glassdrumman river,
and the other stream goes on to the Mill Bridge and
past Ballynahinch to Dromara and Slieve Croob
where the Quoile really starts.

Mr Preston sets out his rod and line and casts to the
middle of the river. The other rod he props against a
stick with the end weighted by a stone, waiting for a
bite. He is then ready to offer advice about bait and
untangling lines and sorting out hooks and picking a
suitable one from the selection stuck into a cork borrowed from the bar and carried in a trouser pocket for
safety. He explains that we might catch roach or pike,
neither of which is worth eating, but pike is very fierce
and if it is a big one, better let it go and lose the rod and
line than be pulled in after it. He hopes one day to

catch a trout, but the trout have been ruined by building the floodgates and dredging the river, especially since in the government's meanness they have not put in a fish pass and the trout cannot get up or down, and the salmon, the great glory of the river, cannot get back from the sea to spawn and now will never return.

Mr Preston never ever caught a trout. I never caught a roach or pike, so we were level in that way, and at the end of the day I would go back through the Mount and over the hill and he would disappear in the direction of Church Street. The swans and the ducks stayed, and the reflection of Inch Abbey on the water and the monks in their limbo waiting for release, and the bell at the bottom waiting to ring and the chalices and monstrances, pyxes and ciboria in the mud at the bottom, and the key to open the cathedral door, all waiting for redemption: for the reversal of the Reformation, the restoration of the monasteries, and a better day.

NINE

MY MOTHER WAS A GREAT BELIEVER IN offals. Livers, kidneys, ox tongue, tripe, oxtail, sweetbreads, we had them all, both from the butcher's next door and from the abattoir, and very nutritious and delicious food they were too. Her great *tour de force*, however, was black puddings which she made to her own recipe with great care and with a devotion to process that amounted to ritual. First there was the bread to be crumbed, not pan loaf but the plain, stumpy baker's loaf, torn off the ticket of four in the back of the van, with the sides raw and gaping, the domed crust overcooked and the bottom burnt tough like the sole of a shoe, dirty and grubby from having been dragged along the floor of a drawer or the top of a counter. First the rough sides had to be squared with a bread knife, the top crust removed and the loaf cut into cubic chunks for easy handling with the tin grater. The trick of grating was to keep rubbing until the whole cube of bread had been reduced to a pile of fine crumbs in the bowl, without leaving any lumps, and without at the same time scrubbing the tips of your fingers against the rough edges of the grater. This was not only painful and likely to produce cuts and abrasions, but it would spoil the breadcrumbs by allowing blood of the wrong type to be introduced to the mixture. I thought it strange, seeing what was going to happen to them later, that the bowl of breadcrumbs should be regarded as polluted by a drop or two of my blood. I developed a technique of holding the bread in the palm of the hand rather than with the fingers and rubbing the last bit with the ball of the thumb, which was broader and flatter than a finger and minimised the risk of injury.

Meantime there were onions to be sliced, sore on the eyes and nose and causing tears to flow, even of any bystander, but this was a job Mammy did for herself. The onions were mixed through the breadcrumbs along with sage and thyme and mixed herbs and whatever combination of spices happened to be at hand or interested her at the time. Then, in a large crockery mixing bowl, glazed on the inside and raw on the outside in a way that threatened to tear your nails off when you handled it carelessly, the pile of prepared breadcrumbs was left to await its anointment with blood.

This had to be procured, fresh and hot, direct from the slaughterhouse and from the throat of the animal. For this I was dispatched to the abattoir in the Shambles with two of Mr Galbraith's gallon cans, scrubbed out and scalded and with lids firmly fixed on.

The abattoir was run by the council and was part of Daddy's empire as town clerk. It provided facilities for local butchers to slaughter their cattle and sheep and it was intended to cut down on the number of private slaughterhouses which were a bit of a nuisance in residential areas, encouraging rats and other vermin. Not all the butchers used it, only the smaller ones. The larger ones like Thompsons' and Lavertys' and Kellys' tended to kill their own cattle and were proud of their skill at doing so.

In these early days, Jack Weighman was in sole charge. Jack was the abattoir manager – a high-sounding title for a very varied role. He was an amiable Englishman from Cumberland who had worked in the iron mines in a village called Frizzington before coming to Downpatrick to live with his mother's people. Aunt Lil said sharply that it was to escape conscription in the Great War. In any case, he had become the council's general factotum and my father's right-hand man. He sat outside the door at council meetings to keep unwanted callers from bursting in. My mother called him Black Rod. He looked after the floodgates at the Quoile, he weighed the pigs on grading day, he trained and led the local fire brigade, and he coped with any emergency that came along. He lived in a small house in Pound Lane opposite both the gates of the infirmary and the site of the old pound, and he was the main person in the town for getting anything done. Jack was my card of entry to the abattoir, and the guarantee of my safety from wild animals and from even fiercer-looking butchers and slaughter men with skinning knives who could get very mad indeed if you got in their way and who used very bad language to advise you to clear off.

The abattoir was at the back of the Shambles, whose name meant a place for killing animals. It consisted of a lairage for animals waiting to be slaughtered on one side of a concrete yard, which was either slippy with shit or drenched with water from having been hosed down. On the other side were two slaughtering pens leading to a skinning hall and then to a cooling room where the sides of beef were hung for a few days before being collected for transport to the shops to be sold. At this time refrigeration was virtually unknown and cooling was effected by draughts of air through louvred vents in the doors and ceilings, assisted by a fan in warm weather.

The animals were brought in overnight, unfed to allow them to empty their stomachs before slaughter. They were driven, some sullen, some reluctant, most unknowing, up through the streets in a small herd by men shouting and banging sticks and thumping rumps with ashplants, and young boys running ahead to block off gateways and to prevent the cattle running down side streets or back alleys. This did not always work, and stray cattle, as if sensing where they were being brought to, broke away sideways and into shops and houses, from which they were beaten out backwards by angry people fearful for their property, or at worst the cattle defiled the doorsteps and walls with watery, pungent shite, forced out by fear: not the placid, perfectly formed platelets of cow clap left by the parading dairy herds in the morning but an indiscriminate splatter of mud and filth, spraying further as it hit the ground and creating a sticky and smelly mess all along the street.

The nearer to the slaughterhouse you went, the more concentrated the noise and the shite and the smell. Cattle and men and young boys all became more confused and congested as they faced into the narrow passage past the Shambles, along the side of Arderin (a terrace of council houses), past the gate of Menowns' farmyard and in through the wide, corrugated clad-iron gate of the abattoir and into the overnight pens.

In the morning, the animals were let out into the concrete yard one at a time, except when one of the butchers, with more bravado, reckoned he could deal with two or three at once. Each slaughter man seemed to have a way of knowing which animals would go meekly to their fate and which might even be dangerous if he did not have help. The animals were first driven or coaxed through a wooden sliding door into a slaughtering pen. This was a room about twelve feet square with no windows but tiled to the ceiling in white tiles, which were cracked here and there where a hoof or a horn had hit them. The floor sloped down towards one corner where there was a gully grate to carry off the blood, and there was a sinister round iron eyelet sunk into the wall about a foot above the ground. The far side of the room from the door had a wide opening into the skinning hall, also with a wooden sliding door, and there was an arrangement of overhead railings with hooks on runners which extended from the skinning hall out into the slaughtering pen.

Once a beast had been got into the pen, a noose was thrown round its neck, and the rope was looped through the iron eyelet in the wall and pulled hard by a couple of men, or more if the beast was troublesome or so scared that it thrashed around and kicked out wildly. The pulling on the rope had the effect of forcing its head down and its body round so that it was brought to its knees with its head near the ground and down near the gully.

The slaughter man then prepared the humane killer. This was a bit new-fangled at the time and was thought to be a great advance on stunning the animal with the blow of a sledgehammer on the forehead, or on simply cutting its throat without any preparation at all. The humane killer was a gun with a hand grip and a trigger and a great fat body. The body contained a steel tube, like a small pipe with a sharpened end, which was driven forward by the charge. For anyone brought up on Zane Grey and the Wild West, it was a disappointing gun. It did not hang easily from the hip in a leather-holster, it could not be drawn, spun and cocked in one movement, it could not be fired from the hip, it did not fire bullets or slugs, or bring animals down on the hoof as they ran with a single shot from a master marksman. What happened was that the charge, in a small brass capsule, had to be put in place before the gun could be fired. This drove the tube forward a distance of about three inches out of the casing. It had a name stamped on the side, CASH – CAPTIVE BOLT PISTOL. No good to Billy the Kid.

When the beast's head had been pulled down and it was on its knees, or on its side if it had slipped on the wet floor or been very rough so that it had been pulled, nearly strangled by the noose, up to the killing place, then Jack Weighman, who had custody of the gun and who had to count out the cartridges from a small cardboard box according to the number of animals to be killed, one for each, handed the pistol to the slaughter man, Bertie Connolly or Bobby Neilans or Hughie McKee. The gun was intended to be used once only on each animal – more would be untidy, unprofessional, unkind, and a waste of bullets. The end of the tube was placed against the animal's forehead, above the eyes, in the centre, the trigger was pulled, there was a bang and a smell of cordite, like a squib going off, and the animal gave a sort of grunt and heeled over. The effect of the sharpened tube was to bore a small hole into the beast's skull through which blood oozed when the smoking gun was withdrawn, its tube protruding and gooey with blood and a white substance. The slaughter man now took a thin bamboo rod about two feet long, stuck it into the hole, and twisted it around vigorously. The purpose of this activity was to penetrate the beast's brain and to make sure that it died quickly, if the initial shot had not killed it off.

Sometimes as a result the animal writhed horribly and threw its hindquarters around so that the hooves flailed. The next step was to slit its throat, or at least to cut open the jugular vein with a sharp knife which allowed the blood to drain out into the special gully which conveyed it to a concrete tank under an iron manhole cover out in the yard from which it could be ladled out into milk churns and taken away to prevent it being washed down the sewer in its raw state. It was at this point that I would present my two cans to be held under a vein to catch the flow of blood as it came out, fresh and red and steaming, to be caught before it clotted, before the cold got at it, not the thick bluey stuff but bubbling red. Then, can covered tight, I would run off down the hill and across the corner in through the yard gate and up the steps to the kitchen where Mammy was waiting with her crock of breadcrumbs to complete the mixing of her black puddings.

The animals waiting to be killed lowed sadly in the pens across the abattoir yard as if, although unseen, they were aware of the fate of their fellow. They were not supposed to see another animal being knocked down and sometimes the cruelty man was around to see that this did not happen. At other times Bertie Connolly was in too much of a hurry, or too fed up, or not anxious to go out of the warm steamy atmosphere of the slaughtering pen into the cold yard, or there was no help at hand, or the animals were light and docile and he brought a couple of them in together to adjoining slaughter rooms.

If you did not have to rush off home with an express delivery of blood to the black-pudding assembly line, you could, if you crouched in the corner beside the winch handle, hang round the abattoir and watch the rest of the work. It was a busy, steamy place with water everywhere, people in rubber aprons and gumboots, steels for sharpening knives hanging on a cord from their belts, and knives everywhere, flashing, pointing, nicking, slicing, knives being steeled and honed, up and down, flank and flesh, flash flash, slice slice, grind sharp-edged, tested on thumb, hostile and menacing.

The effect of the lethal bolt and the poking with the pithing rod seemed to be to remove whatever brakes there were to the animal's natural expulsion of gas and material. Sometimes not quite drowned by the noise of the charge was a grunt and a gasp, a belch and a loud fart. This was accompanied by a flow of piss and a shot of stringy greeny-yellow shite which made the whole place slimy and made walking about difficult even for the men in gumboots so that you were afraid of them slipping and sticking themselves on one of their own knives.

Soon the hosing-down started to clean the floor and walls and flush the mess down the drains. And scarcely had the writhing ceased than one butcher seized a front hoof and began to make cuts. Gradually the hide was peeled away, nick by nick, cut by cut, exposing flesh up to the breast bone. By this time the place had been hosed down and was relatively clean and the stink had been replaced by a smell of meat and sweat. The animal was now on its back, the feet had been cut off and slung in a corner to be carted away for making glue, two cuts had been made in the houghs (the area behind the knees in the hind legs), and a broad steel bar with pointed ends had been forced into the cuts. This thrust the legs apart, exposing the sex and other organs, but giving some stability to the rear end. The bar contained a central eye into which a large heavy hook attached to a wire hawser was fixed. The wire rope was threaded over a series of pulleys to a winch mounted on the wall of the skinning hall, which, if you behaved yourself and kept out of the way of flashing knives or the danger of slipping on the wet floor, or the even greater crime in Mammy's eyes of getting grease on your gansey, you might be allowed to crank up with a huge handle.

This had the effect of pulling the beast, now half-flayed, with half the hide cut away and its hind legs splayed apart by the steel bar, through the open door from the slaughter pen into the skinning hall. As soon as the carcase was through, the wooden door would slide shut, the one into the yard would open, the pen would be given a final hose down, another animal would be brought in to be roped, and the cycle would begin again.

Meanwhile the flaying of the dead animal would proceed. Sometimes, if they were in a hurry, the skinners would continue their work as the beast was being drawn across the floor, with a continuous knife cut from the breast right down the belly and through the testicles to the crotch. The great skill was not to leave any fat on the underside of the hide, which would cause it to putrefy, and not to make any cuts in it either, which would reduce the value for leather making.

The skin is now cut away from the ribcage. The carcase is cut open and the guts spill out quickly and are slit open to allow the contents to be flushed out, a fairly stinking fluid reeking of yesterday's undigested grass, bubbling and boiling, a bilious green, until the contents are sluiced out disclosing the honeycombed inner wall of the stomach and the tripes which are then hung up to dry. The skinning meantime has gone on apace with more of the hide being released by each nick of the knife, exposing ever larger expanses of flank and haunch. Sometimes Bertie Connolly will get hold of a loose end and pull it down like peeling a banana. This continues until the whole carcase is bare; the hide is then detached by snipping the last bit at the base of the skull. Then the head is cut off – the butcher holding on to one horn to steady it for the cut – and thrown in one corner, great mournful eyes staring out unseeing, the tongue is removed and hung on a hook or a wall rack, and other bits and pieces are hung on a standing frame in the middle of the floor, ready to be wheeled away as the final turn of the winch handle brings the carcase up clear of the floor and ready to be split into sides. This is done with a cross-cut saw, right down the middle, dividing the back bone, splitting the carcase into halves which then swing loose, each depending from its separate hook, linked to a wheel on the carrier rail above. After a final, shivering parting and a final hose-down, the two sides are pushed out on the overhead rail through another set of high doors into the cooling hall.

The cooling hall is high and airy and painted white. The floors are dry but streaked with lard so that you have to be very careful not to slip. One of the overhead rails is a weighbridge connected to a big dial like a clock face calibrated round the rim in hundredweights, stones, pounds and ounces, with a single quivering pointer which swings about a bit and oscillates before it settles at a point at which a reading can be made by Jack Weighman and entered in his book. The hall is filled with hanging sides of beef waiting to be ready for removal whole or cut into hindquarters and forequarters, each stamped with a blue stamp to show that it has been inspected and passed. The walls are covered with steel racks with hooks attached, on which are hung banks and rows of sheep and lambs, also cooling and waiting to be collected, and the odd pig, but not very many, because most of the farmers kill their own or send them to the factory.

Sheep were killed on a different day from cattle. They were driven in in flocks, darting everywhere, with men and dogs chasing them and rounding them up as they escaped down the back of Arderin or into

Giblets Rea's backyard or Menowns' haggard, and
bringing them back into the herd, which darted and
drove with a life of its own until they were all pressed
against the wall trying to get through the narrow door
to the pen. The sheep were not roped for killing, just
driven into the slaughter room, two or three or four at
a time, and shot in quick succession with a smaller gun
with a lighter charge than that used for cattle, right in
the centre of the forehead, between the horns, and
then lifted up quickly so that the fleece would not be
stained and ruined, and hung by the back legs from
a hook in the wall. Sometimes, in a hurry, Bertie
Connolly would pick up a lamb in his arms and carry
it, sometimes two – one under each oxter – but that
was only to show off his strength. The sheep were
flayed more easily than the cattle. Once started the skin
just peeled off and was taken out and laid in a pile. The
guts too, the bag and coil of intestines were taken
across the yard to be cleaned out, first by squirting
out the remains of the shit or whatever was there, then
having the outside cleaned by being pulled against a
thin piece of wood held in the hand by Mr Duddy
which scraped off the scum and the fat, the whole time
under a flow of tepid water until the gut, yards long,
was clean and flat and coiled like a fishing line in
hanks, steeped in brine and hung up on a hook to dry.

Killing pigs was an even more complicated affair, as
they had to be scalded and scraped to get the bristle off.
The pigs squealed a lot and ran everywhere between
men's legs, sometimes knocking them over which
made them curse and swear, sometimes seeking refuge
under tables and benches and having to be prodded
and hooked out. Usually a pig was finally caught in a

corner, sometimes with the head of a yard brush shoved against its jaw to keep it penned against the wall and to keep its head still enough for a moment for it to be despatched with the humane killer. Then the pig would be hung up and bled before the carcase was dumped in a great iron cauldron of scalding water heated by a hose line of steam from the boiler, its gauges trembling and threatening to blow up, and the fire roaring when the door was opened for more coke to be shovelled in. The pig had to be scraped all over and the bristles floated in a scummy mess on top of the cooling water, after which the pig was taken away and hung on a hook in the wall to have its in-nards removed.

On black-pudding-making days, the can of blood I rushed home with would be swiftly mixed with the breadcrumbs into a thick, gritty paste. This had to be put into a casing of sheep's gut, also picked up in the abattoir. Mammy would take a tin funnel, a tundish with a broad nozzle like the ones for putting fuel into motorbikes, or paraffin into hurricane lamps, but a bright clean special funnel that she kept only for this purpose, made specially for her by Mr Galbraith the tinsmith who lived at the bottom of Bridge Street. The whole thing had to be scalded and then greased before the gut was loaded on to the outside of the noz-zle and pushed up and up, fatter and fatter, larger and larger, until only a little bit was left hanging. This was knotted with slippery fingers to close the end. Then I held up the funnel with two hands, and Mammy ladled the bloodied breadcrumb paste with a wooden spoon into the broad part of the funnel, stopping every now and then to poke the handle of the spoon down the hole to make the mixture flow more easily. My job now, as well as keeping the funnel upright, was to keep a grip on the gut so that it slipped gently and evenly off the nozzle, and not too quickly, so that it filled up nice and plump with the paste, producing an ever-lengthening blood-red sausage of impressive thickness and evenness, with no empty spaces and no small air bubbles and unbroken as it coiled under its own weight until Mammy decided it was long enough. Then, a length of gut would be snipped off, cut with the scissors, and knotted tight against the filling to produce a solid, compact cylindrical column of pudding.

All that remained was to coil it in a large stockpot, cover it with salted water, and boil it until it was firm and black. Then it could be taken out and cooled and sliced off in discs like large black washers and fried in the pan for breakfast, along with the slim which Auntie Lil made from cold leftover potatoes mashed up and mixed with flour and water, rolled out flat with a rolling-pin and baked on a griddle on top on the range.

TEN

THE DOWNPATRICK RACES WERE RESTORED IN 1938 after not having been run for years. By then the racecourse had become run-down and dilapidated. Daddy said that the course before that one, the Old Course, was the best course of all and should never have been given up. Daddy had a book which said that the races had been started in 1685, by permission of King Charles II by the Down Royal Corporation of Horsebreeders which ran them there for years until they were stolen away from Downpatrick and transferred to the Maze, near Hillsborough. We went for a longer walk than usual one Sunday to see the Old Course, over Irish Street, out past the iron horse trough against the infirmary wall, past the planting where Alex John O'Prey from Killough had crashed his bicycle and broken his shoulder, avoiding the steepness of Racecourse Hill, past the graveyard and the bad corner at Kellys' where all the cars crashed which had left a permanent hole in the railings.

The right turn at the Flying Horse, which Daddy

said was the name of an old inn, brought you to the beginning of the course, which was a broad grass laneway with hedges along both sides and a narrow dusty road running along one side. Clumps of whins were invading the grass, but you could see that it had been a track of some sort, and there were hoof marks where somebody had been galloping horses on exercise. The track extended for a mile or so and then ended in a sort of turning circle for the horses to run round and get back on the track again going in the opposite direction. This was the Course-end, near the road to Killough, indeed nearly halfway there. Our own route took us back past Ballymote on the long road home.

On the Sunday before the races resumed at the newer racecourse, we went out to walk the course, as Daddy called it, which lots of people did, to inspect the fences and the jumps and to walk round the mile and a half of the course between the white-painted posts and rails, marvelling at the fences with the white wooden rails leading in to them, the jumps themselves made up of bound bundles of twigs, tied together and fixed to a rail. There were regulation jumps too, which were higher, with a ditch on the take-off side and a drop on the other, and a water jump where a drain crossed the course. There was talk of the old days, of a four-day race meeting and the crowds thronging the town and trains coming in every ten minutes, and people milling out of the station and jarveys and sidecars and jaunting cars and the hotels full and the pubs doing a roaring trade and every knacker in the country and every crook and trickster in town, and card sharps and three-card-trick men and trick of the loop and pickpockets and side-shows, and all the bars with extensions and tables and benches on the footpaths and in the yards, open round the clock, and drink through the night and up in time for the first race and on and on for the four days. And stout having to be brought in on the train every day and porter by the wagonload and whiskey too, and God knew where some of it came from and how much poteen was filled into bottles with better labels that it deserved. And Major Beamish up there in Vianstown and Mrs Beamish, a better rider than any man, who won all the point-to-points on the trot, and Waring Willis and all the horses that went on to win at Punchestown and Fairyhouse and even at Liverpool. But the course was not right, switchback, going the wrong way round, no straight, too easy at the start, too hard at the finish, would kill the best horse, and the fences not stiff enough either.

There was an excursion to the station on the Tuesday evening to see the horses come in. Old-timers moaning the days when there were trains and trains of horses, wagons stretching out to the loop line, specials with special looseboxes, and every stable and loosebox in the town full for the week. Out past the station, past the East Downshire coalyard, in at the gate past the pig-weighing station where Jack Weighman operated the scales every Tuesday, sliding the brass block along the swinging bar until it was level, and shouting the weight out for Fergie McGrady to write it down in his book. We went past the cattle-beach and on to the horse-beach, a raised ramp with buffers mounted on sleepers sunk into the bank, and a flat gravelly platform for the wagons to be unloaded. After a long wait and many false alarms and looks up the rails towards the loop line, the rails started to hum and an engine with wagons came in and backed painfully through the points, Paddy Wylie hanging out of the signal-box window to make sure everything was right, and the driver handing in the staff, the baton that allowed the train to proceed to the next section of line. The wagons bumped to a halt, and then, after a minute or two, the bolts were knocked aside, the flaps were let down, and the doors swung open. Now the horses began to emerge, beautiful leggy thoroughbreds, pawing lightly at the top of the wooden ramp as the stableboys and grooms encouraged them to come out, pulling at the headstalls, rubbing their noses, patting their shoulders Then the horses emerged a little bit more, the plated hooves grating against the slats on the ramp, then there was a bit of a rush and a run down the ramp to the flat bank, the boys having to run a bit to keep up. All the knowing people were able to identify the blinkered horses from the initials on the corner of the rugs cinched tight on their backs, and were busy seeing which one was quiet and which frisky, which one sweated too much and which did not sweat at all, and running round and looking for tips and decoding nods and winks from the stableboys and giving information silently out of the sides of their mouths as all plotted and planned to beat the bookies the next day. Mammy said not to pay too much attention: none of the punters had motor cars, while Tommy Breen and Willie Tweedie, the bookies, each had one.

Daddy had a badge that let him in to the races and two smaller ones which he gave to Malachy McGrady and me. We walked out with him along the footpath, past the jarveys and jaunting cars at the station, which were waiting at the big cast-iron horse trough for fares. They picked up five or six people each and dashed out the Ballydugan Road to the course, the passengers' feet sticking over the sides. The visitors wore hard hats on their heads, some with glasses in a box slung over the shoulder, some with baby Powers to the head, the bottle thrown away empty over the hedge into the marshes; others were bookies with bags and stands, rushing to get there on time. We walked in a steady stream of people, past the Market Yard and the Fair Green and the stinking gasworks, and the dump which smelt worse, over the Plank Drain and out, the crowd getting thicker, the pace slower, as we approached the racecourse. There were horses being walked in and out of the crowd. Better to keep a respectful distance in case they would lash out with their feet, or rear up, or bite. We picked a careful way too past the steaming lumps of horse manure that sat in globules, shining in the sunlight, all along the road and footpath. Through the turnstiles, showing the magic badge, into the broad, gravelled area before the stand. Up the steps to the old stone part, a view back over the marshes to the cathedral and into the town, the crowds thick on the road now, the stragglers from the pubs running to get there in time for the first race, the jaunting cars, too, caught up in the throng and reduced to a walking pace. Out the other way, across the course, you could see the Mournes, the train pulled up at the special racecourse stop beside the bridge on the Killough line, and people scrambling up the bank and into the stand and the silver ring out on the other side of the course.

There was a beautiful little black horse on display

called Workman. It paraded along the front of the stand before the big race. It had won the Grand National in 1938, although it did not look big enough to tackle the regulation fences at Downpatrick not to mind get over Becher's Brook and the other giant fences at Aintree. But I didn't voice my doubts: I didn't suppose they would say it if he hadn't done so.

We found it hard to take much interest in the races themselves, apart from looking at the horses in the parade ring and finding a bookie who would take threepenny bets. That aside, it was all horses falling and being brought down, and loose horses cantering wildly among the others and putting them off, and men running out to catch them by the reins and missing, and one horse lying on across the brush fence and having to be shot, the sound echoing round the course, and jockeys lying still as horses jumped over them, and the long wait wondering would they ever get up, and the relief when they did and limped back up the course. The excitement, then, as the horses appeared from behind the trees and started to come faster down the hill and people craning to see what colours were first, and the thunder up the hill to the winning post, and the shouts and the cries and the yell of relief at the end of it all, and people tearing up betting tickets and throwing them away in disgust, and others rushing to the bookies on the cry 'Winner all right!' to collect their winnings. There was one horse, in front, running away with the race, which veered off the course up the lane to its stable to roars and shouts of, 'And what would you expect?', and 'It's all a racket anyhow'.

On the way home, we walked with Mr Johnston, the solicitor, who talked to Daddy about the opening of the Phoenix Park racecourse in Dublin in 1902. The first race, he said, was won by a horse called Dunbarton Rock, and the band of the Dublin Metropolitan Police played selections from *Maritana* under the trees. It all seemed more stylish than our trudging in the Ballydugan Road on a darkening autumn evening.

ELEVEN

BEER CAME IN BARRELS, LARGE ONES CALLED hogsheads, lesser ones called kilderkins or firkins, and little ones called pins. The beer and stout usually came by train to the station and were delivered round the town by Fitzsimonses' horse-drawn dray. It was very difficult to manage the great hogsheads which had to be slid off the dray along parallel wooden rails which had an iron hook that clipped on to the side of the cart. Some people rolled the barrels down the slope thus created, but this was risky as a barrel could run away from the men who were holding it, or run over them and hurt someone, or bang against a wall and stave itself so that the beer was lost or damaged. This was all right for the firkins or kills (as the kilderkins were known for short) or the little pins (which could actually be lifted off the dray by a strong man) but even these could run away and might break an ankle if you were not careful. The best way for a hogshead was to take it end first, the belly of the barrel lying in the groove between the two rails, and edge it, inch by inch, down the slope until the iron rim touched the ground and it could be rolled away or spun along on its edge into the bottling store. The Transport Board, which sometimes delivered the beer by lorry, was lazier. Their drivers carried a couple of large bags filled with sawdust like great beanbags, which they threw down on the ground at the side of the lorry and simply bounced the barrel down on to it. Mammy did not like this because it shook up the beer so that it had to sit longer before it could be bottled, and because she liked the Fitzsimonses for their helpfulness and civility and wanted them to get the work.

Bottling was an important and continual activity. First the bottles had to be washed, which was my job and Frankie's. The empty bottles came down from the bar in shallow wooden trays, each holding two dozen, a mixture of beers and stouts, taken down by Ray first thing each morning or last thing at night. They had to be sorted out to separate our bottles from those of commercial bottlers who supplied special beers and lagers, Patz and Pilsener from Bavaria, or Tennents or Whitbread from England. These bottles were mostly the ones with the new-fangled crown corks which we called tin-tops, which were collectable by schoolboys for some reason.

We bottled Guinness from Dublin, Smithwick's from Kilkenny, MacArdle and Moore's from Dundalk, and Caffrey's which was brewed in Belfast. All of them were Irish brands. Bass, Worthington and Whitbread were English beers, pale ale, the labels said, and they were bought in from a wholesaler in Belfast whose lorry came round once a week to leave in new supplies and to collect the empty bottles.

The sorted empties were stacked in crates eight or ten high against the wall; Ray could add to the stack simply by throwing a box of empty bottles up, but Frankie and I had to make a platform of upturned empty boxes to stand on. The dregs of the bottles were drained into a bucket for Mammy to use to fertilise her geraniums which she grew in boxes, pots and beds up and down the steps and around the back door. Once emptied, the bottles were stacked row upon row on top of each other in a great galvanised tank which held seventy-two dozen bottles, enough for a hogshead. When the tank was full, or there was enough for Frankie to be going on with between his other jobs, or for me to do after school, the tank was filled with boiling water from the tap, scalding hot to scour and sterilise the bottles, but sometimes so hot that a bottle or two cracked or split. When the water had cooled just enough to let you put your hands in without scalding them, the bottles had to be taken out one at a time and the water had to be shaken out of them, glug-glug back into the trough, sometimes using a small round bristle bottle brush, with a little loop on top to hang it up by, which you could stick your finger in to pull the brush up and down inside the bottle. Some-times wine bottles, or port bottles if they were en-crusted or had been left for a long time, or beer bottles with slime and sludge in them, had to be cleaned with bottle shot, a handful of lead pellets put in through the neck and shaken vigorously up and down, which was great fun, until the glass inside was clean.

Bottle washing made the skin of the hands very soft and crinkly and liable to be easily gashed if a cracked bottle broke exposing a sharp edge. This could give you a bad cut: the blood would pour into the water, and you had to hold the wound under the cold tap to clean it, the water as cold as you could bear to staunch the flow of blood. Worst of all were the thin slivers of glass that floated in the water, sharp as needles, and could pierce a finger or a thumb, or the fragments of thick glass with an edge like a lance which lurked on the bottom to be met when you were searching for the last bottle or two in the murky water, darkened by lees and sludge and full of floating labels that had detached themselves from bottles and which had to be scooped up and squeezed out and thrown aside, and which often concealed a jagged fragment of glass or a broken bottle bottom which could lay open a finger to the bone.

The scalded bottles were laid carefully in a tank of cold water to be rinsed and then taken out and stacked upside down to dry in a special rack made by Willie McCracken (who had made my cart in Killough). The slatted shelves up to head height held about 120 dozen bottles. After the hot water, the cold water of the rinsing tank was a shock; a hand that had been red and soft quickly became blue and chapped on a cold winter morning, and sore and tingly too if you were prone to chilblains.

Bottling was a great ritual. First the hogshead had to be rolled up on to a low stile or bench with two cross-beams hollowed out to cradle the swell of the barrel. The stile had room for two hogsheads and a couple of rests for smaller barrels. This was a job for Ray, sometimes with help (which was often less an aid than an encumbrance) in rotating the barrel so that the bung hole on its flat (now vertical) outer end was at the bottom exactly in the middle. To prevent the barrel rolling off, two little wooden wedges were hammered in on either side and it was left to settle for a day or so before bottling.

Next the tap had to be prepared, a beautiful brass piece which had been sterilised by boiling in a pot on the kitchen range. It had a long tapering tail, fluted and grooved at the sides and with holes all along the shank to let the beer out. The smooth part of the shank, between the spigot and the holes, was sealed with a washer made by wrapping a strip of carefully folded and wetted brown paper in an intricate pattern of overlapping folds around the barrel of the tap. This was a carefully judged and skilled procedure. Too much paper, or not finely tapered off, and the tap would not go in far enough to clear the perforations, or the paper would bunch and burst and leave open channels for the beer to seep through. Too little paper, too thinly wrapped, and the tap would shoot straight through the bung and the beer would pour out. Once the wrapping had been completed, and without giving the paper time to dry out, the tap had to be held in the left hand, tapered end against the cork that sealed the lower bung hole, dead centre, perfectly level and absolutely straight. The trick then was to strike one powerful blow with a heavy wooden mallet held in the right hand, of sufficient strength to drive the bung inwards and to propel the stem of the tap rapidly inwards too, so that the paper washer was compressed and sealed the outlet. If this was done perfectly, there was a pop, a satisfactory hiss of gas, and a few beads of foam could be seen around the rim of the hole. If it was less than well executed, beer could spurt out across the room and gush until a couple of hefty whacks on the end of the tap drove it home. A badly delivered blow, or a tap that was not straight, or a badly prepared wrapping, was a disaster. Worst of all was a tap with a loose spigot which flew open with the force of the blow, leaving beer gushing out, foam and spray everywhere, and gallons of precious stout and all the profit of the barrel lost.

The bottling apparatus was primitive in the extreme. A rectangular copper tank on a cast-iron frame was placed under the tap. From a bar along the top, eight long brass pipes were swung like slightly deformed penises, through which the beer was delivered to the bottles. Below, a cast-iron frame with ledged shelves held the bottles steady.

The copper tank was filled with foaming stout from the tap and the idea was to create a siphon in each of the swinging pipes so that the liquid would flow up out of the tank and then downwards to fill the bottles. To start the siphon in each case it was necessary to suck the hole on the long end until the liquid started to flow. This gave you a mouthful of raw, rancid, immature stout which you wanted to spit out quickly, and needed to if you didn't want to have the runs for a week. Once the beer started to flow, you loaded a bottle on the end and went on to the next one.

When all eight siphons had been got going, the job was to take each bottle off the tube just as the stout got to the bottom of the neck and replace it with an empty one. Once a good rhythm had been established, it was possible to replace bottle eight just as bottle one was filling up, and to keep a steady flow on the tap out of the barrel. Sometimes one of the tubes clogged or there was an airlock, or the siphon was broken and it was necessary to suck it to start it up again. The frame holding the bottles was sitting in a shallow tray to catch the spillage, which could then be recycled through the copper tank; when the flow from the tap slowed down there would be a delay while the barrel was vented or spiled. This was done by boring a hole with a gimlet in the broad bung on the top side of the barrel until the air hissed out. This speeded up the flow from the tap, which could be controlled by tapping in the pointed wooden spile which was used to close the hole.

Most of the bottling was done by Ray with Frankie and me as assistants. Frankie would bring the empty bottles from the drying rack in low trays and take away the full ones on the other side. My job in this production line was corking, which was messy too at times, but at least you didn't have to suck on a siphon and risk swallowing down some of the stuff.

Corking was done on a machine that had a heavy, cast-iron frame and a huge pedal which you worked with your foot, flexing your knee and standing on tip-toe to get a purchase on it. There was a round brass slot into which you placed the cork, and a wooden thing below like the buffer on a train on which you placed the bottle, with the neck directly below the brass slot. When you pressed the pedal with your foot, the buffer rose to press the neck of the bottle firmly against the bottom of the brass slot, and at the same time a rod of polished steel, of exactly the same diameter as the hole in the slot, rammed down into the slot and forced the cork into the neck of the bottle.

The corks were special. They came in large square sacks and had to be of good quality, otherwise the stout would get corky or the bottles would leak. They were dry and hard and smelled of bark. Ray said that was because they *were* bark, stripped off trees that grew in Portugal. Before they could be used they had to be steeped overnight in a bucket of boiling water, covered with a sack to keep the steam in, and left to soften until they floated to the top. As a result of this treatment, the corks which before had been hard like wood became soft and pliable and rubbery.

There was a rhythm to the work of corking once you found it, a case of filled bottles at waist height on the right-hand side and a bucket of corks in hot water on the other. You lifted a bottle with the right hand and placed it on the pad. At the same time, with the fingers of the left hand, you fed a cork into the slot, one of a handful grabbed from the bucket and kept in the palm of the hand, then you pressed on the pedal, shot the cork home, put the corked bottle back in the case and started the sequence again. As time went on you could get really quick so that the motions were nearly simultaneous. But there was a danger if you pressed the pedal too quickly of nipping the top off a finger while you put in the cork. Pressing too slowly, or too softly, on the pedal would drive the cork only halfway in and you would have to draw the cork and start again, breaking up the rhythm.

There was the risk also, if you pressed too hard, that the bottle could break in your hand, spraying stout everywhere and leaving you with a bad cut.

The corked bottles of the young stout were carried off to be binned, and that was the nicest job of all. First of all it was not in the cold bottling store, but in the real store, which was under the sitting room and warm and cosy, sharing the heat of the house, kept at an even temperature so that the stout would mature slowly. The bins were a range of brick-built compartments with vaulted brick roofs. The bottles were laid on their sides on a bed of clean sawdust, with the corks outwards, in a neat row, three parallel rows to each bin. A full row would be covered with sawdust and another row of bottles laid until the bin was full right to the top and right out to the front, when more sawdust would be spread on top and a label would be placed on the front to show how many dozen there were and when they were bottled. Depending on the weather, it might take three days or a week for the stout to be right and then it could be brought out and the sawdust dusted off and the bottles labelled and stored standing upright on the wide wooden shelves above the bins.

But the best times were when I was sent in to the bar to relieve Ray for his tea. I sat there, listening to the gossip, pulling the odd stout on the chrome hand cork-drawer mounted on the mahogany counter, pouring it out, glass held at just the right angle, the black liquid flowing gently along the side, then tipping it up so that the foam rose to the top, and sinking the neck of the bottle into the foam so that the extra flowed back inside the bottle and not down the outside of the glass, and did not upset the collar of creamy froth which settled solid and serene on the top of the glass like a Roman collar as the tiny bubbles rose through the liquid. Or pouring out a half-one of whiskey in a pewter measure, careful to fill it up beyond the standard mark and not to give short measure, and not to overflow or spill, but the measure held over the tumbler just in case, and then toppled over with a flick of the wrist into the empty glass, the cork put back in the bottle, the tumbler pushed across the counter with a jug of water new-filled from the tap, money put into the drawer. In the drawer there were round wooden bowls, one for silver, one for copper coins, and a space for ten-shilling notes and pound notes in between, and the big white tissue-paper fivers hidden away by lifting one of the round bowls. Or whiling away the time by washing glasses at the copper sink and placing them on the draining tray below the counter, and taking up the washed glasses and drying them with one cloth and polishing them with a softer one so as to bring up a bright sheen.

Sitting on the high stool inside the counter, I pretended to read a book or newspaper, ready for another order, not wanting to appear to ignore a customer, not wishing to butt in on conversations or to appear to be listening. The old man from the courthouse, sitting morosely in mid-afternoon, his lunch-time drink having extended to this and wiped out the rest of the day, getting more and more sorry for himself as he mumbled half-remembered snatches of poetry:

> Sunset and the evening star,
> And one clear call for me,
> There'll be no moaning o'er the bar
> As I put out to sea.

Then, in a moment of lucidity, 'Not a bloody murmur. There's gratitude for you!'

Or Mr Johnston, fresh in from the Petty Sessions, in triumph at having got somebody off on a charge of having a lightless bicycle with bad brakes, recounting past cases in minute detail. Telling the story of Chief

Baron Palles coming to the assizes and staying with
Miss Quarrel in the Judges' Lodgings up beside the
old gaol and being taken in a carriage to mass each
morning. And his horror at having to try a case of
bestiality. Or Skin the Goat and the Invincibles after
the Phoenix Park murders being escorted in chains by
the soldiers of the Devon Regiment, up English Street
to the new gaol past the door of the house Mr Johnston
had lived in as a little boy. The prisoners had been
brought by boat from Kingstown to Dundrum and
did not know where they were until they heard a girl
speaking with a County Down accent, when they said
'Thank God we're in Ireland anyhow!'

Mr Johnston also remembered as a young solicitor
in Wallace's office going out to Strangford to help to
make the will of the old Baroness de Ros; hers was the
oldest baronetcy in the English peerage, transmitted in
the female line. Quite unusual, he said. She lived to be
a hundred. Did you know, Maurice, that she danced
with the Duke of Wellington at a ball in Brussels on
the eve of the Battle of Waterloo?

And the pride of knowing about Waterloo, and
being able to tell Mr Johnston about Thackeray and
Becky Sharp and the Duchess of Richmond's ball,
read about in a book borrowed from the Carnegie
Library and consumed under the blankets by torchlight. And wonder too at being able to talk to a man
who had talked to a woman who had danced with the
Duke of Wellington – at getting back to Waterloo in
two lifetimes.

Sometimes too I heard things I would rather not
have heard. A group of Protestant men sitting in
the back lounge, the door partly open, discussing

Mammy and Daddy. He was all right, they said, but she was too sweet, a Southerner with a Kerry accent, never know what they're thinking. Couldn't trust them. Poor, poor Mammy. So anxious to be fair to everyone, telling us to judge people as we found them, trying hard not to take sides, and all she gets from people she thinks of as friends is ignorant suspicion and hostility.

There was a man too who used to boast about his wife's beauty even though she had bandy legs. 'Legs out of it,' he would say, 'Mary's the best-looking woman in Downpatrick.' We all called him 'Legs-out-of-it' and people who smiled politely and agreed with him laughed at him and mocked behind his back. Aunt Lil told her version of his boasting to somebody one day as 'Legs apart . . .' and people laughed even more. I couldn't see why. For me, she had spoiled the story.

There was another man who said he would never fight with his wife no matter what she said or did. He would kiss her arse for peace. Mammy christened him 'Peace-by-ordeal'.

On a race day I might be sent up to the dining room when people were sitting on after a late lunch and James Blaney wanted down for his dinner, in case a crowd of scruffy cyclists was tempted to steal the silver. One day I was joined by a crotchety doctor who talked with great interest until he became irritated by the bad language from another table and fixed them with a disapproving stare. One of them snarled over in a strong Belfast accent, 'What are you looking at us for? What's wrong with us?' To which he responded mildly, 'Speaking as a medical man, I'd suggest rickets.'

There was a man who used to come for tea some

afternoons, after visiting a patient in the hospital, which he did faithfully for years. The man's name was Mr Yeames, and his father had painted a famous picture called *When Did You Last See Your Father?* In it a group of Roundheads are questioning a little boy standing on a hassock. I went to look at the picture among the prints on the school walls, and remarked on the likeness between the old man and the child in the painting.

Mammy and Auntie Lil often talked about Kerry and about Dublin before the war, when no respectable woman would walk on the GPO side of Sackville Street, and how it was destroyed by bombardment and Mammy had to flee. And the people who used to come to the hotel where Mammy worked, supposedly to have tea but really to plot the rebellion: Tom Clarke and Thomas MacDonagh and Sean MacDermott who had a limp but was the finest-looking man she had ever seen. All this made figures from history appear as human beings, though they were careful not to glorify them in case it would give romantic young boys the wrong notions.

One day I brought home from school a biography in Irish of Cathal Brugha, whom Mammy had never been able to place. His photograph was on the front cover, and when I said it was Cathal Brugha, she said, 'Nonsense, that's wee Mr Burgess from Lawlors' the candle-maker.' Somehow he never seemed so fierce after that.

If bottling beer was a ritual, bottling whiskey was high mass. This was celebrated by Daddy inside the house in the boxroom on a wooden table covered with a white cloth. The whiskey came mostly in five- or ten-gallon crockery jars protected by wicker basket-work with a handle on each side for carrying. There was also a crockery loop as a handle near the lip of the jar itself, and a cork which was covered in red sealing wax and stamped with the seal of the distiller to make sure that nobody had interfered with it in transit. In any case, Daddy had a glass instrument called a hydro-meter to test the strength of the whiskey and to make sure that nobody had watered it. There was Jameson's, Dunville's and Comber, all Irish whiskey; Scotch whisky, spelt without the *e*, came already bottled in wooden cases with a wooden lattice to separate the bot-tles. Daddy said the Scotch whisky was only blended, but Irish whiskey was the real thing. It was good to be able to say from learning Irish at school that whiskey meant *uisce beatha*, the water of life, or from Latin *aqua vitae*, which made bottling it an altogether serious and solemn job, great care and reverence to be taken, not a drop spilt.

Daddy always began the bottling ritual by carefully removing the sealing wax from the top of the cork of the whiskey jar, trying to take it off in one piece and wiping the rim of the jar before pulling the cork in case any of the red wax went into the whiskey. The cork, a large bung about three times the size of a bottle cork, was drawn with a corkscrew. The whiskey was then poured out into a jug sending fumes all over the place, and filled carefully through a funnel into clean, clear ten-glass bottles. Daddy filled them carefully right up to the neck, about an inch above the shoulder, and set them aside for corking. He would only do about six at a time before corking so that the whiskey would not evaporate; the jar had to be corked quickly between each fill of the jug for the same reason. Even so, you could smell whiskey at the top of the stairs and right down into the boxroom. The corks used in the bottles were longer than beer bottle corks and of better quality, but they had to be steeped overnight in boiling water too. Daddy did not use a corking machine – which would risk breaking a full bottle – but pressed the cork in by hand and drove it home with a sharp blow of a special wooden mallet he kept for the purpose. Sometimes he filled half-bottles or half-pints or naggins (which held two glasses), and sometimes I was allowed to fill out the little glass bottles using a smaller funnel and a small jug of whiskey filled from a bottle. As the whiskey was taken from the jar, it grew lighter so that Daddy could lift it up easily, and he poured the last jugful by holding the jar upside down to drain out the last few drops of the precious liquid.

Whiskey did not have to be binned, but labelling took a lot more care. First there was the capsule, a lead cap which was placed over the cork and which was moulded to the shape of the bottle by looping the lace of a football boot around it and pulling it back and forward and up and down until the ridges in the glass showed through the lead. The capsule could not then be removed without breaking it: the bottle was sealed. Then there was the large label with the brand name in gold embossed letters which had to be carefully pasted and fixed exactly in the centre of the bottle and smoothed down and wiped off, and a small slip underneath, and a crescent-shaped piece with three stars which had to be placed like a necklet just below the neck where the bottle swelled out. Daddy said this was called the etiquette.

The only Irish whiskey that came in a bottle was Bushmills. The distillery provided nice advertising water jugs shaped like the Giant's Causeway which were always getting stolen. Mammy said people were awful, even the best of them. If they had only asked she would have given them a jug. Although I'm not sure, she might have given them another, but I don't think she would really have given away a Bushmills jug except to somebody special like Mr Johnston, or maybe Bertie Brown, who would not have wanted one anyhow.

TWELVE

MY MOTHER WENT TO 7.30 MASS EVERY morning, walking up Irish Street, stopping at John Doris's window just below the police barracks, where the steepness of the hill was beginning to get to her, glad of the excuse to appear to be doing something sensible rather than just aimlessly gathering her breath. As a result of which she did something that was not sensible at all, staring at rows and rows of bland, boozy faces photographed grinning ritualistically at dances in the Canon's Hall or the town hall or wherever. At times she would sigh and ask why couldn't they sort things out so that she could just amble up English Street to the cathedral and say her prayers there. An ecumenist before her time, she nevertheless prayed freely, fervently and frequently. She embraced other faiths too, being careful to spread mayflowers, which we had been sent to gather in the marshes, on the windowsills on May Eve, to keep the fairies away from the home, and on the roof of the byre to protect the cows. She was also superstitious, and careful about breaking taboos and about when and in what order she did things. If she was particular about a letter she would send John Cross to post it because he was a bit simple and therefore lucky. Daddy was always sent out just before midnight on New Year's Eve to first-foot her so that a dark man would be the first to cross the threshold and enter the house and handsel her for the new year and bring us all luck.

Weekday mass was a sort of penance for all of us. I was allowed to sit at the back so as to be able to duck out quickly and run home for breakfast so as to be in time for school. My exit was supposed to be at the last gospel, which would normally be frowned upon, but got earlier if the priest was slow or started late. Sometimes, instead of running down the hill, I walked round the Circular Road with Frank Cunningham (going to do his day's work in the East Downshire coalyard) and his wife (going down for the *Irish News* to read the death notices in case some of her family or friends had got away unknown to her) and Ray too. And I would listen to Ray and Frank exchanging news, gossip and improbable stories.

Sunday meant a double visit to the chapel, to mass in the morning and back for holy hour in the evening. Oddly enough we thought the Protestants were very religious, overdoing it in fact, as they marched soberly up to the cathedral or the parish church with their hard hats and gloves and their large Bibles under their arms and the unfortunate children marched off to Sunday school while we went out to play.

Normally our church was a low-key affair. The church was bigger than the little chapel in Killough, but still a chapel just the same, with men and women on different sides. There was a little corner called Our Lady's Chapel with a bench along the wall where Daddy sat most of the time beside a large statue of Saint Patrick, dressed in vestments like a bishop, with a mitre and crozier and holding up a sprig of shamrock in one hand as he taught about the Trinity. This bench was very cosy because the heating pipes ran behind it and you could lean your back against the wall. It was reserved for older men, who would glare and mutter and not move up or straighten their knees to let a cheeky boy in. So you could not sit beside Daddy and had to find a seat. The church's main altar was white, large and carved, with soaring spires and a recumbent Christ being laid in the tomb on its front, much grander than Killough. There was a pulpit too, which would never have been heard of in Killough where the altar was good enough for anything the priest had to say. The pulpit was a big stone tub up against the pillar with carvings on it of Saint Patrick chasing the snakes out of Ireland. Auntie Lil said he hadn't got them all, there were still a few left, making trouble and cheating people. High up in the walls were stained-glass windows which made it all very mellow, and a huge window like a wheel over the choir at the back, which was beautiful when the evening sun shone through it in September and sent shafts of coloured light, with the dust dancing in them, shining across the seats and along the walls. What made it more beautiful was if the door was open and the white light of the evening sun flooded in at the same time. There was an old nun in the convent called Mother Brendan who told Carmel that her father had designed the chapel and that the windows had come from Munich in Germany and the altar from Germany too.

Downpatrick did not go in much for high mass. The less dramatic but still musical *missa cantata* was good enough for the Canon and did not take so much manpower. Still, there was plenty of ritual: colourful vestments heavily encrusted with gold, green most of the time, purple in Lent, red on martyrs' days, drab black and white for requiem mass, and gold for sung masses. We knew the names of all the bits and pieces: the amice, the alb, the surplice, the stole, the maniple and the chasuble, and the gold-lined vessels, the chalice, the pyx, the ciborium and the monstrance. For benediction there was a heavy gold cope to be draped across the shoulders of the celebrant by the head altar boy, and long red and gold stoles, and black birettas to be handed to the priests at the end so that they could march in procession on and off the altar carrying the chalice draped in the same cloth as the chasuble, the altar boys going first, led by the cross-bearer and followed by the thurifer swinging incense. And all the time the Latin intoned:

Introibo ad altare Dei.
Ad Deum qui laetificat juventutum meam.

Benediction, like high mass, was an assault on the senses. Then the altar would be banked with candles, far beyond the thin meagre ones for morning mass, or the six tall ones, three on either side of the tabernacle, lit on a Sunday morning by an altar boy using a taper on the end of a long pole, trying hard to get them to light first time, knowing that his skill was on trial before the whole chapel. For the big occasions the altar was covered in flowers in tall brass vases, daffodils in spring, tulips in June, gladioli tall and flaunting, and, on the great days, wide-open arum lilies or languid lilies of the valley. Behind the flowers and above them were banks and banks of candles in sloping brass candelabras, higher and higher, raised up on wooden blocks until the altar looked like a mountain in flame when the teams of altar boys with their long poles had liberated the wicks into light, the topmost ones first so that they did not burn their hands, and then down to the bottom, past the table of the altar to other candlesticks placed on the floor of the sanctuary.

And there was the crash of the organ, and the choir with one glorious voice soaring over all, and the smell of incense as the thurible was swung and brought down again and opened and the seeds of incense were sprinkled on the burning charcoal with a brass spoon from a brass urn, and the lid of the thurible closed down in a rattle of chains and the clang of metal meeting metal, and handed by the thurifer to the priest to be held up and swung back with one hand, bouncing against the chains, clang, clang, clang, and sending clouds of scented smoke which hung in the air and stung the nostrils.

But the nicest smell of all was at the end if you had the patience to wait, or were held up as the crowd filed through the narrow doors, or you had to wait while Mammy said extra prayers for something or other, for somebody's exams or that Ray would get a job, or to Saint Anthony to find something she had mislaid, or to Saint Jude because it was all becoming too difficult, or to Saint Joseph of Cupertino or a dozen others who happened to be in fashion. While you waited, the altar boys would come out again to snuff the candles with a tin cap on a long pole, starting at the bottom this time and working up to the top, having to go back for one that had guttered into life again, and leaving a smell of hot wax and burnt wick and acrid decay. The noise of the thurible being emptied outside the sacristy door let you know that there was another smell to be savoured outside as you went home past the glowing embers in the grass beside the vestry steps.

Sometimes the ceremonies went on for days on end in what was called a Quarant Ore or Forty Hours' Adoration. Then the chapel was left open all the time with the monstrance on the altar and people were told off in relays, street by street, to be there through the night, and visits had to be made through the day and the lights got brighter and the music louder and the candles higher and more splendid and there was no time for the incense to clear between services so that it built up and filled the sanctuary and floated back into the nave in a grey aromatic fug. The great thing was that you could be late for school on these mornings and that was an added attraction.

After a while, not being an altar boy and not able to sing in tune, I found a steady job pumping the organ. The organ was up in the gallery where the choir sang, with pipes of varying thicknesses and heights almost blocking out the great rose window, and a keyboard and knobs and pedals and a high bench. There the nun sat to play the organ, with her back to the congregation and a little rear-view mirror above the keyboard to one side to let her see what was going on at the altar.

The organ had to be pumped to make it work, by means of a long shaft like a blacksmith's bellows sticking out of the casing. This shaft had to be moved up and down to keep the pressure up. The pumping was a plum job: it ensured a seat even when the church was most crowded, you could sit on the floor if necessary, it was warm, with a good view of what was going on, you could even nod off if the sermon got boring, or read a book, but you also had a sense of contributing, of being part of the ritual, of producing pressure just at the right time to enable the organ to come in on cue and the choir as well.

Once a year there was a mission, a great blood-and-thunder revivalist sort of crusade, with a week for men and a week for women – who presumably had to be told a different set of truths. Since the sixth and ninth Commandments and sexual sins and adultery were high on the missioners' repertoire, I presumed that they could not be discussed in mixed company. The priests came from two orders mainly: the Redemptorists who came with a big wooden cross with a gory Christ on it which they put up behind the pulpit, and the Passionists who wore big black cloaks bearing a white motif in the shape of a heart with a cross on it. Claire called them the 'passionate fathers with their loose habits'. Mostly they had Southern accents which gave them a slightly exotic flavour, and they spoke of overseas mysterious lands where they had been on the mission, and how much better the Catholics were there, or in the town they had been in last week, than we were in Downpatrick. Sometimes Mammy or Daddy would know who they were or know their people if they were from Waterford or Kerry, but otherwise they were visitors from outer space.

The sermons contained much talk about company-keeping and the evils of sex. Much of this was above our heads, but caused the older boys to blush or giggle or nudge each other in the ribs. It was all about pure young Irish girls being led astray and ruined in the cities of England and America – something that didn't seem to happen in Ireland – and left in the gutter to repent just before they died, and the dangers of lonely roads and crossroads dances (of which we had no conception) and riding in the backs of cars (of which there were very few in Downpatrick), and the wickedness of modern dancing (which went on every Sunday night in the Canon's Hall nevertheless), and later the utter depravity of jitterbugging and the sinfulness of crooning, the wireless and most of the pictures we saw at the Grand cinema. It was a long list and very hard to keep up with, and most of it was outside our experience anyhow. On the way out you would hear one of the young bloods saying, 'You won't get a leg over tonight while the mission is on.' Whatever that meant, apart from riding a bicycle.

The church would be crowded with forms along the side aisles, with benches too on both sides of the centre aisle and seats around the altar and sanctuary and people standing up the middle and around the doors. The missionaries came in pairs and worked the hard cop soft cop routine with one being gentle and persuasive and the other a roaring and ranting scold. And since you had to go to confession during the mission, and since it would be cheating to go to one of the local priests, there were always long queues outside the box where the soft cop carried out his interrogations.

The final evening, the closing of the mission, produced a crescendo of noise and emotion. Everybody had to take a wax candle with them, or buy one on the way in, which you left on the seat afterwards to be used on the altar. Just before the benediction, and after another stirring sermon, the priest would invite people to renew their baptismal vows, taken on their behalf by sponsors or godparents but now to be personally underwritten and validated. Everybody stood up with their unlit candle, with a bit of paper wrapped round the bottom to prevent hot grease running down and burning the fingers, then you lit your candle from the candle of the person next to you until the whole church was a sea of flickering flames, faces appearing and disappearing in the fitful light. Then, at a command, candles were held high above heads and the shout rang out: 'Do you renounce the world?'

A mumbled 'I do!' was not enough for the missioner. 'Louder! Louder! I want it to resound around the hills of Down. I want it to be heard in the streets, right up to the cathedral over there on the hill, right round the world. Do you renounce the world?'

'I do!'

Louder! Louder! Louder!

'Do you renounce the flesh?'

'I do!'

'Louder! And the sins of the flesh, and the evil thoughts and the fornication and the adultery, and the sins of lewdness and perversion, and the flight from chastity and the lusts of the flesh, and Hollywood and the movies and dirty books and pictures, and bad women and lewd girls and those who would lead you astray? Louder! Louder! Louder!'

'I do! I do! I do!'

'Do you renounce the Devil?'

'I do!'

'Not loud enough. Is that all you can do? Is that the

strength of your faith? Is that all the men of Down can say? I want to hear your shout. I want it to echo round the halls of heaven. I want God to hear your loyalty to him, I want your suffering Saviour on the Cross to take comfort from it, I want it to re-echo in the caves and caverns of hell for the Devil himself to hear. Satan! Lucifer! I will not serve! Deny Him! Deny Him! Louder! LOUDER! LOUDER! Hold your candles high. Hold firm to the faith, be a light shining in the world, a beacon of belief in a stormy sea of wickedness ... Louder! Louder! Louder!'

'I do! I do! I do!'

With the decibels mounting, the final feral roar was like the sea in storms, a drum roll before battle, a cry of defiance to the world, the flesh and the devil: 'We do! WE DO! WE DO!'

'You can put out your candles now. Be careful how you snuff them and place them carefully on the ledge of the seat in front of you.'

After that, benediction was a release, a renewal; we went out into the night drained of emotion, Christian soldiers, confraternity men for the fight – but with no very clear idea where the enemy was except that he lurked everywhere, ready to devour the one who broke ranks.

We were sent on our way with the strains of 'Faith of Our Fathers, chained in prisons dark, and yet in heart and conscience free', and not knowing that they were not good Irish martyrs from the penal times, but English fathers who had nothing to say to us at all.

These were the excesses, however. Most of the time, religion was more humdrum. The Canon was the essence of practicality and no-nonsense. A strong-minded man, he demanded obedience and dominated everything in the parish and the town. Most things were associated with him, the Canon's House, the Canon's Hall, the Canon's School, the Canon's Dam, where we played impromptu football and hurling when it was dry, and where we skated when it was frozen over. The Canon had to keep control of every-thing and was said to be particularly concerned with money and with keeping up the level of collections. Jimmy Quinn said the Canon could never die because there was nowhere for him to go. There was a boss up above and a boss down below. The only place the Canon could be boss was Downpatrick, and there he would stay. The Canon was, however, very plain and approachable and very charitable in his own gruff way although he would not let on to it. His sermons were generally short and to the point, mainly because he had been giving the same ones for years and years. My favourite was the Christmas sermon about the vil-lage schoolmaster and organist out in the snow in the Alps composing 'Silent Night' in German. We could all repeat it nearly word for word, and follow old Herr Grüber up his mountain in Ober Salzburg (where the Canon had visited to see for himself), where he sought inspiration and a means of substituting music for a broken organ. Then the choir would begin to sing 'Silent Night' and we would all shout our heads off.

One chore at Christmas from which there was no escape was helping the Canon to put up the crib. The cave was built in the side porch by fixing crumpled black paper on a wooden framework to simulate rocks. The Canon sat there like a big child, having to crush every sheet of paper himself to ensure perfection. Then he personally supervised the placing of the figures in the straw, the infant in an imitation manger, the ox and the ass and the shepherds decently waiting outside the entrance of the cave, and a great tinselled star nailed to the ceiling for the removal of doubt.

The Latin mass did give you a sense of belonging to something that was bigger than Downpatrick or Ireland and that was worldwide. It was also an insurance against persecution and penal days. We had powerful friends out there and up above, even if they did not always seem to be interested in our problems. We were told that you could go to any country in the world and mass would be just the same, as it had been down the ages, and this was the great unifying bond. There was a great sense of community too in just being there, the church full most of the time at mass and devotions, people standing at the back and round the doors and spilling out to the top of the steps. Then there was the buzz as the crowd dispersed, and the chat and the gossip outside the door, and moving down the street in a band and not feeling alone or unsupported.

Confession was a weekly ritual, queuing up for your turn, trying to think of sins serious enough to confess while being frightened of chastisement for those you did admit to, and comparing penances and lengths of stay in the box, or the degree of interrogation or the crossness of the confessor. Mass lasted an hour, and if you went in after the first gospel you were late and had to go again. To leave before the last gospel was another crime, unless in an emergency. There were novenas for this and that which meant nine evenings on the trot, and Nine Fridays, which involved mass and communion every Friday for nine weeks in succession, and all lost if you missed the eighth. There were November Devotions and May Devotions and Lenten Devotions and Advent and Saint Patrick's Day and Corpus Christi and Sundays and Holy Days of Obligation and almost anything else anybody could think of, and the Men's Confraternity once a month and the Women's Sodality and the Perpetual Novena every Friday night so that there seemed to be few days in the year on which we did not go to church.

Jimmy Quinn thought that a lot of this church-going, especially by women, was hypocritical. 'Look at them,' he would say to my mother of the Children of Mary in their blue cloaks, 'eating the altar rails. They'd cut your throat behind your back.'

Offerings at funerals were a particularly sore point with Daddy because the amount given by each mourn-er was read out in the presence of the dead person's relatives and to the whole congregation. This reading out was done in relation to all church collections and stipends, but Daddy found it particularly distasteful at funerals because it seemed to put a price on the worth or popularity of the deceased.

Oddly enough, in those days Saint Patrick's Day in Downpatrick was really not such a great occasion, although we were very proud of Saint Patrick buried up there on the hill with Brigid and Colmcille. He was ours and we would claim him, and we were not going to give him up. Neither did we believe the rumours that he was British. That would have been too much to bear. After all, we were civilised and had people like the Red Branch Knights and Celtair of the Battles (although he could be crude enough at times) and bards and druids and mighty heroes when the British were painting themselves blue with woad. And it was from Ireland that missionaries like Colmcille went to convert the British from paganism, so the British could not possibly have converted us. All of which convinced us that as well as having died at Saul and been buried in Down, Patrick had been born in France. Had to be; after all, that's where he headed for when he escaped. There was no second way of it. Also it was a pity that his grave had been stolen by the Protestants who didn't really believe in him, along with the cathedral and Inch Abbey and all the land about.

Building up to Saint Patrick's Day there was a novena, culminating in a Forty Hours in the chapel at which we all belted out 'Hail Glorious Saint Patrick, dear saint of our isle' as the last hymn each evening, getting better at it and singing louder and louder each successive evening of the novena until on the morning of the feast day it became a triumphal roar. And Father McCluskey would get up and start his sermon with 'Here, in this church, the head and mother church of all the churches in the English-speaking world . . .' and we would all feel very important and well-connected both in heaven and on earth.

But Saint Patrick being up in the cathedral grave-yard was certainly a bit of a dampener. You couldn't make a fuss up at the grave, which was virtually ignored on Saint Patrick's Day. Indeed, most Down-patrick people ignored it most of the time and only went up there to show it to visitors who then let you down by hauling out rosary beads and blessing them-selves and things you shouldn't make a show of yourself doing in a Protestant graveyard, in front of Protestants, and maybe giving offence as well. I always tried to distance myself by going over and scraping the moss from the O'Laverty gravestone with my shoe, and pretending to read the Gaelic inscription on it.

On the Sunday before Saint Patrick's Day there was the expedition in search of shamrock, trying to remember good places where it had been before, and trying not to be fooled by clover. Joan was the best judge of the genuine article, which didn't grow anywhere else in the world but Ireland, and was best found on the slope of the field behind Fanny Breen's garden and the old barracks, and which had to be dug up by the roots with a dessertspoon carried in the pocket for that purpose, and brought home and passed by Daddy as the real thing, and washed and kept floating in a basin of water. On Saint Patrick's Day there was a sprig for everybody's lapel, small and neat and not the great bush that some people put on their caps. Apart from that, the day was dull. The shops opened, but for some reason the pubs were closed, to prevent the Irish getting drunk and fighting, it was said, but that did not prevent a few people coming into the bar behind drawn blinds, to drown the shamrock, they said with a laugh. Saint Patrick's Day was in Lent, and if you had gone off sweets for Lent you could gorge yourself all day, right up to midnight if you were still awake and had not already made yourself sick.

If you wanted to sit in Saint Patrick's Chair, the place to go to was Struell Mountain, out behind the asylum, a good walk, too far for a Sunday mostly, but good fun to go to in a crowd on Struell Night.

This was Saint John's Eve, Midsummer's Day. The first stop, down the long muddy lane at the side of Kellys', was Struell Wells which had been blessed by Saint Patrick. There was an old stone church, a ruin with no roof and grass growing on the floor, just three walls and a gable where you went first to say a prayer, and then across to the wells. The first two were little stone beehives with steps down into them and clear water at the bottom. The first, which was round, was called the Drinking Well. It was supposed to have a cure for all sorts of sicknesses and hurts and there were pieces of rags tied to the tree beside it, left there by people who were said to have been cured, and hanging off a branch, a small wooden crutch made for a child. The next well was square; it was called the Eye Well because the water there cured diseases of the eye, and people knelt down and cupped water in the palms of their hands and bent their heads to bathe their eyes, or steeped handkerchiefs in water and stouped their eyes with them, the water running down their cheeks like tears and dropping off their chins, to be wiped with the back of the hand and shaken away. Oddly, there were no old pairs of glasses hanging beside this well.

Then it was on to the bathing wells, the women's and the men's, oblong buildings with stone-slabbed roofs and two great tanks with water flowing through them and holes that could be stoppered to make them fill like a bath. There were niches in the wall for holding clothes and keeping them dry. Nobody tried bathing on Struell Night, although some paddled in the stream in their bare feet.

Then we would stop to read a metal plaque which told how the wells had been repaired and preserved by

Lady Betty Southwell, then go across Davy McClean's guttery farmyard, stopping to look in at the sow wallowing in the mud, but avoiding Davy in his chair at the door in case he might growl at you, and up over a stile in the loose stone wall, pushing aside brambles and ploughing through ferns and bracken on the narrow worn path that led up round the shoulder of the mountain to Saint Patrick's Chair.

Struell Mountain was only a hill and in any other self-respecting place with real mountains it would not have been noticed at all, not to mind called one. Compared to the great peaks of the Mournes, our Alps, it was a molehill, but here on the lower land, just because it pushed a few feet higher than the other hills around and was not cultivated to the top but was covered in whins and provided a view of the sea, it was a mountain. Up the side of the hill a single file of people shuffled, looking for the chair, and there, round the corner, it was: a flat slab of stone with another at the back and two at the sides like arms, and there you had it, a solid and compact and not very comfortable chair, but good enough for a saint who was not into easy living anyhow, and good for him to sit on and to survey the countryside and to see the sea where he had sailed up in his little cowhide coracle, and think maybe of France and of being captured as a slave by Niall of the Nine Hostages. The chair was a solitary sort of place, and even though the asylum was just over the hill and the town was just beyond that, it felt lonely and even for a moment isolated from the people standing around or those scrambling down or those waiting to get up.

If you sat in the chair and wished, or said a prayer to Saint Patrick, or maybe both, the saint would look after you and you would get what you asked for, although after the effort of going up the mountain it was hard to think of something to ask for that would be worth the trouble or that would not trivialise the opportunity, so you generally didn't ask for anything at all. There was more of a rush of young girls to sit on the chair, because if they threw three pebbles over their left shoulder and wished right, they would see in a dream the person they were going to marry.

After the ascent it was all a bit of an anti-climax with people standing around talking and laughing, and the light going but never quite disappearing so that there was no real darkness, and wondering how long you could safely stay out without getting into a row at home, and walking back in a band along the asylum wall and wondering whether to go home by the roads or take the shorter but wilder route over the Gallows Hill which was rocky and rough and full of potholes but which plunged dramatically down into Scotch Street which you could run down and get up enough steam to race across the town hall corner in the semi-dark and up the last lap home.

The old men grumbled about the great Struell Nights in the past which went on till morning with bonefires, as we called them, which people jumped through because it was midsummer, and dancing till dawn on Struell Green, and tea and maybe something in it in Davy McClean's, and lying in the grass, and all innocent fun and coming home in the morning light for breakfast and off to your day's work. And all stopped by the priests who did not like dancing or see-ing people enjoying themselves, and all for a drop of drink, and what if there was the odd row, sure it happened at football matches too, and all the old customs were going and what a pity, and Struell Wells should be better looked after, and the priests didn't do much about that because the Canon wanted all the money for himself and wanted the dances in the Canon's Hall, and look how he carried on when Jack Weighman and Joe Moore and a few of them ran a dance in the town hall for the infirmary, but it was a great night all the same. And the priests did not like the people coming out on Struell Night to say a few prayers to Saint Patrick, and some of them should be here to say a rosary or something – but maybe they were as well off without them, having a smoke and a bit of crack.

With all that, you had the feeling that Saint Patrick was more likely to have been at Struell than either the cathedral or Saul. Saul, one mile to the east of Down-patrick – or two depending on whether you measured to the Protestant church or to the statue – and where Saint Patrick had died, was where the main Catholic ceremony was held, but not at Saul itself where there was a Protestant church with a fake round tower – very nice all the same, but not the real thing. On the gatepost on the upper road there was a stone with a large key carved in it. Claire said the key had been hid-den there by the monks when they had been cleared out of the cathedral. I thought that Carmel had said it had been flung into the Roughal and wondered how it had got up to Saul. Maybe it had floated up on the water.

Arthur Pollock said you had to imagine the Quoile as an inlet of the sea, and water all around Down-patrick, if you were to understand how Saint Patrick had sailed up and landed there in the first place, and in any case he had landed at the mouth of the Slaney river which was where the Fiddler's Bridge was on the Strangford line. Maybe it was a duplicate key and the monks hadn't wanted to throw both in the river but to hide one in another place. But the key in the stone was a bit of a fraud. It was not hidden at all except that you had to rub the moss off with your fingers in order to see the outline of the ring at the top and the stem and the wards, and it was far too big to fit into the key-hole in the door at the end of the cathedral behind the high cross which was the one the monks were sup-posed to have locked for ever on their way out.

For Catholics to remember Saint Patrick there was a huge statue on the top of Slieve Willien, which had been rechristened Sliabh Padraig, which seemed a cheeky thing to do. Like renaming the Circular Road St Patrick's Avenue, which very few people in Down-patrick ever bothered to call it. The day the statue was opened or blessed or unveiled or whatever they did with it, which was shortly after we came to Down-patrick, we were all brought down by Claire and Joan through the hotel yard and out the back gate, down the steps and along the narrow passage beside the cinema, to stand in the rain on the footpath outside the Munster and Leinster Bank. The covered part under the canopy where you queued for the pictures was filled by people who had been there all morning. Mrs Fox, who had a religious repository on the other side of the road which sold rosaries and crucifixes and scapulars and pictures of the Sacred Heart and holy pictures and icons and mass cards and blessed candles and brass candlesticks and holy-water fonts with angels on them, had a big white and yellow flag hanging from an upstairs window with crossed keys and a funny hat on the white part.

After a while standing in the drizzle, everybody got down on their knees and a black car came slowly up the street with a little old man in the back wearing a white lace surplice and a scarlet skullcap who blessed the people as he went along. Joan said this was Cardinal MacRory who had come from Armagh to bless the statue. I wondered if he had seen on the way the phantom team of oxen with Saint Patrick's coffin which had fooled the Armagh men, who wanted to bury the saint in their town. Claire said he was not as ugly as Cardinal Logue which didn't seem to have much to do with the blessing. Then we were up on our feet again, as he disappeared round Breens' corner, and up the narrow gauge and back through the gate and running up the yard to dry out in front of the range in the kitchen.

Daddy said it was a frightful waste to spend all that money on a statue when there was not a proper school for boys in east Down. Mammy said never mind, the school was there now, wasn't it? Daddy said that wasn't the point, the money could have been put to better use.

You could see the statue from the Quoile and from the golf course, huge and standing there on its hill. The awkward thing was that the ceremonies were not held on Saint Patrick's Day but on a Sunday in June. Mammy said it was because March was too cold for the Bishop to come out, and anyhow it was in Saul and Saul was a strange place, and you needn't go anyhow and very few from Downpatrick would take much to do with it. And this brought down stories

about Saul and the parish priest, Father Rhodes, who
was a funny little man, but very kind, who played golf
every day with Willie Smith, the schoolmaster, and
waggled the club fourteen times before he hit the ball.
And about the auctioneer who cried out when he got a
very low bid for a farm, 'Saul, Saul, why persecutest
thou me?' And the same auctioneer, a man called
McGrath from Portaferry, being told off by the
Reverend McElnea whom he had tried to get to start
the bidding for a big iron cauldron – 'It would make
a fine bell for the Presbyterian church' – only to be
told, 'It would, Mr McGrath, if it had your tongue in
it.' And Father Rhodes, complaining of being called
out at night unnecessarily for a man who was not seri-
ously ill: 'And when I got there, where was he? He
was in bed with his wife. Where I should have been.'
And the Saul parishioner, listening to a tirade from the
parish priest about the poor level of stipends compared
to the cost of running a house and a car, who com-
mented, 'A cheaper man would have done us.'

Saul was a slightly exotic adjunct to Downpatrick,
close at hand yet remote and mysterious, full of dealing men, where you could get a bottle of poteen if you
knew where to look. The best time to go to Saul was
not on Saul Sunday which was a bore with processions
and tedious sermons and the Bishop saying mass and
the wind flapping the canopy and blowing out the
candles and muck underfoot. It was better to go out
on the bicycle, negotiating the hairpin bends of Saul
Brae, brake blocks burning and squealing, fearful that
they would go and mindful of the disasters and broken
bones of comrades who had come to grief there, past
Leo Hayes's, who, Ray said, held the bottle of stout

three feet above the glass when pouring it out so as to get some sort of a head on it. Then up the steep hill, flattening out past the chapel and Mr Smith's little ivy-covered house and the school, to the broad gravel sweep at the side of the road. There, bikes would be hidden behind the wall, or just left lying on the gravel, then it was up the grass past the stone altar, on up the narrow path. The great thing was not to look round whatever happened, to keep your head down, eyes fixed on the grass, feet slipping and lungs bursting, to keep on and on, not to stop, and never to turn round until you could touch the base of the statue.

Then to turn round and face the glory of the view. The whole of County Down nearly, like a basket of eggs, hill after hillock, stretching out towards the Mournes and Slieve Croob and right up to Belfast and Cave Hill and Divis and Scrabo tower, and the Quoile glinting as it appeared and disappeared among the drumlins until it widened out at Jane's Shore and after the floodgates to the Quoile Quay and the Steamboat Quay and the woods of Portallo and Finnebrogue and Shooter's Island and Gun's Island and Delamont woods and on out to Killyleagh and Shrigley chimney and the lough stretching back up to Comber and Newtownards and the islands, three hundred and sixty-five of them, one for every day of the year, and the glint of sea on the other side of the Ards, and Ailsa Craig on a clear day, and the Mull of Kintyre and sometimes, exceptionally, Cumbria on the far horizon. Or was that just a cloud formation? And round to the other side to see Strangford and Portaferry and the narrows as the water raced out past Kilclief, and Ardglass and Killough and St John's

Point and the lighthouse, and Dundrum Bay and the Mournes sweeping down to the sea.

The base of the statue was made of great granite blocks, cut square and built higher than you could reach up, with the welt of Saint Patrick's boot just appearing over the edge, or maybe it was a snake he was standing on before kicking them out of Ireland. The statue itself you could just see by lying on your back on the grass and looking up at a stern-looking man with a huge head and a beard, with a crozier in his hand, staring towards Cave Hill. Daddy said most of the work was done by men called McCrickard from Ballymagreehan who were great stone men although a man from London called Doyle Jones had got all the credit and most of the money. Set in the sides of the base were small oblong bronze plates with little pictures of Saint Patrick lighting the paschal fire and converting Dichu who had owned the barn below in Saul, and at his death being blessed by Saint Tassach whose church was in ruins now in Raholp. And you could follow the route of the funeral, drawn by oxen along the river to Down, and the road where the magic oxen went on to fool the Armagh people until they disappeared at Kilcoo and left them all lamenting, but too far away from the burial to do anything about it.

Inch Abbey was another holy place. You could just see it across the Roughal from the back of the Mount. There was said to be a way across when the river was low, and a proper ford further down at Jane's Shore at the back of Kary Hill, across to Portallo wood, but you wouldn't try it, and anyhow the bottom of the Roughal was full of holes and there was that tunnel across to the cathedral that you might fall into. So there was nothing to do but take to the road, over Bridge Street which Daddy's old map called Nun's Gate, past Hughie Green's little gospel hall, past Rathdune where cross old Mrs Crawford was still guarding her precious branches, past Minnie Martin's meadow, past the embankment which Artie Pollock said was a road started by Lady Betty and never finished, past the war memorial with its poppy wreaths, with the statue of a soldier with a rifle and bayonet on top, carved by Tommy Hastings, monumental sculptor who made the headstones for the graves, which Daddy said was so awful that when it was unveiled an old soldier in the crowd had dropped dead. Down past Kary Hill where Mr Perceval-Maxwell lived, past Portland gates and dotty Mrs Pinkerton with the floppy hats, and Albert McGifford's gypsy caravan and treasure house, along the low wall and round to the bridge with the two little whitewashed houses jutting out to narrow the roadway on both sides so that cars could not pass and buses had to edge round, almost scraping the gable walls, and past the houses below the road which were rooted right in the water when there was a flood. Daddy said they were toll houses where coaches and carts had to pay to use the bridge. Then it was round to the left, past the entrance gate to Finnebrogue, and a fearful dash to peer over the wall at the ghost pillars, standing lonely and ivy-covered and out of place among the trees, serving no purpose, on no road or path, having no gates, just two square pillars of cut stone. Claire said they had been built as an entrance to the estate with fine iron gates, but that every night at midnight, when the gates were shut and bolted and barred, a ghostly carriage with six black horses would drive up at a gallop and the gates would disappear. After replacing the gates a few times, the Maxwells got fed up or frightened or both and put up new gates with a gate-house a few yards down the road and they never had any more trouble. The problem was, you see, that they had stolen the stones for the pillars from the ruins of Inch Abbey and they could not have any luck. The pillars were there to prove it. Why would anybody build gate pillars where there was no road, put no gates on them, and then build a stone road across the front to block them off. It was not a place to linger in case the coach would come thundering back or an angry old monk would come out of the trees to punish sacrilege.

There was a signpost against the wall, a fingerpost with the sign pointing up the Cottarhill Road saying in black letters on white, INCH ABBEY 1. Daddy thought this was a funny sign because it really said one mile to the Inch. He said this was the exact opposite of the scale on the folding maps in the bookcase which were one inch to the mile. He said it would make a very big map which would not fold up at all, or go into the house not to mind the bookcase.

On the other side of the road there was a little iron swinging gate, like a turnstile, which you could only squeeze through one at a time. This led you to a short, steep muddy path through the trees which brought you out on to the Cottarhill Road. Then you had another walk through the muck and cow clap and down another lane and the entrance to the abbey.

Larry Lynch, an eccentric science teacher, having walked a group of us out to Inch Abbey produced a missal and began to intone a Latin hymn. Only one boy, Pat, knew the words but we busked along anyhow in mock Gregorian chant. Mr Lynch said that was the first time the Te Deum had been sung in the chancel since the Reformation and he made us say a decade of the rosary for the monks. He also said that ruined monasteries like that were the 'bare ruined choirs where late the sweet birds sang' in Shakespeare's sonnets. I thought it was far more romantic to think of real birds having flown away for the winter leaving the trees leafless and bare, but I supposed he had a point. On the way home he stopped at Mrs Smyth's shop and bought chocolate for the boys who had travelled in by bus, but not for the town boys. I thought that was very unfair.

THIRTEEN

OING UP TO THE OFFICE WITH DADDY WAS A
special treat. Out the front door, past Mr
Thompson inside his picture window, the
tiled heads of sheep and cattle on the walls behind
him, rails loaded with whole sheep carcases and cuts
of beef, he standing behind the counter with a string
of sausages in one hand as he raises them up from the
dish in front of him for the inspection of the lady at the
counter, the other hand with a carving knife poised to
cut when she gives the nod or he thinks the weight has
been reached, but delaying the cut to wave with the
knife a greeting to his friend passing on the street outside. Then into Johnny Moore's for a paper. The *Irish
Independent* for Daddy so that he can follow the fortunes of Count Curly Wee and get news of any death
in Waterford, and the *Daily Mail*. Mr Moore standing
blue-faced, blue-cardiganed and blue-fingered in winter, his neck wrapped in a muffler, a cloth cap on his
head, grey shirt sleeves sticking out through holes in
the elbows of the cardigan, his fingers sticking out of

knitted mittens, pieces of toast, crumbs and butter sticking to his moustache as he lays down a mug of tea to pick up and fold a paper from the piles riffled out and laid in layers on the front edge of the counter, only the titles showing. The whole place reeked of damp and soggy paper and was heavy with the smell of paraffin oil.

'Nice day, Mr Moore.'

'What's nice about it?' And a grumble and growl and a groan about the state of the world and how cold it is, or how hot it is, and the little shop either freezing cold in winter despite the paraffin oil heater sending out fumes, or stoving hot in summer when the door was tightly shut. There were papers, papers everywhere with Molly helping her father and keeping the money right, and Joan Moore (until she went off to join the air force and became a WAAF in a light-blue uniform) and people tramping in and out and ringing the little bell on the door as they opened and closed it.

Down then past Mr Clarke, ex-policeman married into a pub, as he comes white-aproned out of the entry door with a case of empty bottles, and Mrs Clarke and Mrs Skeffington too, sisters, inside the screened window, dusting up after the night before and getting ready to open up, and Johnny Skeffington, slipping out to his butcher's shop in his grey shop coat, and Mrs Holland, who teaches Carmel, leaving her bicycle in before facing up the hill to the convent. And past Hugh Neill's butcher's shops and Mr Telford's shoe shop with the remains of a printed sign across the top of the wall: LONDON BOOT AND SHOE STORE. Mr Telford for some reason was called Gaunch, a tired-looking man with a droopy moustache. He kept a sort

of morning parliament which included John Gray, the
draper next door, and Hugh Dickson from the hard-
ware store round the corner, and Mr Gifford and
Skimmy Smith from the solicitors in the big three-
storey building across the road. And Daddy would
stop to gather the news and hear who had died, and
who might soon do so, before facing up the hill to
the office.

Past Breens' corner with the lines of men, unemployed, waiting to sign on at the Buroo in English
Street, just across from the hotel, and another line leaning against the bank wall, and another at the town hall
corner, sheltering from the breeze in Scotch Street,
and another group yet at the post office corner and at
the foot of Bridge Street. Men everywhere with nothing to do, men waiting for the pubs to open, or the
bookies', men with no jobs and no prospects and
nothing to do but mooch about all day and kill time
and stay out of the house and make the best of it.

Then past Mrs Bell's little shop down below the
slope of the road, a cheery good morning and past
the Horse and Hound bar with Tommy Dougherty
outside, a dapper, jockey-like little man in a swallow-
tail coat and jodhpurs and leggings with a hard hat and
a cravat.

'Good morning. Nice day. Could you lend me a
half-crown?'

'No, Tommy. Good morning.'

'Thought not. Thank you. Nice day. Good
morning.'

Daddy goes into McCartneys' second-hand furniture emporium to see Sam Ross about the possibility
of buying a bed or a wardrobe or a sideboard or a

dressing table for the hotel, best of mahogany, lovely oak, French-polished, not a scratch on it, no wood-worm, take out the drawers, look at the dovetails, not a nail in it, not a mark on it, cheap at the price, don't let it go, it won't be here tomorrow. The Missus will never forgive you. She'll maybe come up herself.

Past Mr Grant, the tailor, tape round the shoulder, chalk in hand, eyeing you for size, ready to cut out. Louis arranging bolts of cloth in the window where the sun would not fade them. Past John Doris, and the police barracks with Sergeant Lowry, who has a rich Limerick accent, opening the gate in the morning to let the cats out of the yard. Past Barney McCartan's barber's shop and across the road to the pub of Pat Forde, fat and flushed and moustached, an ex-policeman and boxer and looking like both, past the Cup and Saucer, a hanging tin sign for a cheap café, and up the steps to the office. The office was in a nice old building which had been renovated after having been used for years as a wash-house. The steps up to the front door were still referred to by the children who played on them as the laundry steps.

In the office, when the door opens, there is a fine fire in the grate, set by Jack Weighman. On a nail over the mantelpiece hangs the now out-of-date calendar with the picture of a black cat on it that Mammy and Carmel and I had brought for good luck the first day Daddy worked there. Daddy, taking the great big key out of his pocket, pulls back the iron flap protecting the keyhole in the strongroom door, puts the key in, turns it, lifts and heaves and pulls the great iron door out on its pivots to release a smell of must and fusty papers and discloses the great rate books on their racks,

and the ledgers stacked on shelves, and bound minute
books with their handwritten pages going back to before the Famine, and chits and bills and cheques and
invoices and banker's orders and drafts and receipts.
Taking out the largest ledger, he opens it, about six
foot wide on the broad, low table, and begins his day's
work.

There was the thrill of being allowed to help, and
reading out the numbers as he checked off the rate
payments into his great book, first moiety and second
moiety, poor rate, town rate and water rate, struck
and determined, assessed and evaluated, calculated on
the poor-law valuation and net annual value with dis-
counts and rebates for agricultural land and railway
running lines, rates levied but irrecoverable, vacancies
and arrears and written-off. Or stamping the street
names on the rate receipt books and demands with a
rubber stamp, making sure to get it level and in exactly the right place and not to smudge and not to get
ink on the page or on fingers, and not to overrun the
page and have to rule it out, and learning the street
names – Pillar-well Lane and Kelly's Entry and Gaol
Wall and Folly Lane and Pound Lane – and sometimes
not the names we always used – St Patrick's Avenue for
Circular Road and John Street for the Shambles, and
Lower John Street for the Gullion and Fountain Street
for the Back Lane, and Edward Street for Asylum
Road. And calling out names for the Juror's List or the
Register of Electors, Resident occupier, Resident occupier's spouse, Company voter, Business qualifica-
tion, Imperial only, Young voter, until all the names
had been gone through and checked over and a good
job done and the cat on the calendar still smiled away.

Then with a penny over to Mrs Skeffington for sweets, or to Mrs Connolly's for what was not allowed, a currant square, a flies' graveyard, Claire called it. Or a jam tart or a Paris bun or a jam sponge which Mrs Skeffington would cut in half for you if you said you only had a halfpenny, then off home, zipping down the back ways, across to Scotch Street through Mary's Lane and Fountain Street and down the hill and home.

Instead of going home you could decide to explore the council yard. There in a large covered shed was a wooden hand cart with high sides and a framework mounted on it to hold a few rolls of canvas hose with brass couplings on the end, a standpipe and hydrant and a few lengths of rickety wooden ladder. This was the town fire engine, to be used in an emergency by the fire brigade, led by Jack Weighman and consisting of the other council workmen, Jimmy Hampton and Dessie Mahon, who were called surfacemen, and Willie John Lowry who normally drove the horse and cart. This was very primitive equipment, of not much practical use in a fire except to reassure the citizens with the appearance of activity. In any case there was generally a water shortage, so the hoses and standpipes would be useless. Most fires were chimney fires which were just allowed to burn themselves out, dowsing the town in a shower of sparks and smuts, or fires in haylofts and barns which were more serious. These were generally tackled by men passing buckets of water from a convenient well from hand to hand along a human chain, but these fires generally burned themselves out too.

The rest of the store and the yard was covered with rusty equipment, higgledy-piggledy, one thing on top of another. There were stencils in large capital letters for painting STOP and SLOW on the roads, and wooden frames for marking out white lines on the road with special quick-drying paint. There was a tar boiler and tar barrels, and braziers and rusty rollers all in a heap, and piles of sand and stones and screenings and grit and dust.

There was also a collection of winches and pulleys wound around with rusting steel cables and wire ropes which were said to have been left behind in settlement of a debt by somebody mysteriously referred to as 'the German'. This man had been given a contract a couple of years before to try to improve the chronically bad water supply by scraping out the main pipes from the Tannaghmore reservoir. This he did by putting a sort of torpedo into the pipe with a wire attached to it and letting the force of the water carry it along. When it was pulled back on the wire, blades would open and rotate, scraping the rust from the inside of the pipe. There were bits of old pipe cut across to show what it looked like, filled with a thick growth that almost closed the pipe up and reduced the bore so that you could scarcely push a pencil through the hole in the middle.

Jimmy Hampton was a great man about water and he was a genius for finding leaks. This he did by placing a wooden stick on top of the stopcock and listening to the other end of it. Sometimes, in order to hear better, he would lie down flat on his face on the road and put his ear to the ground. He was nearly run over once or twice by cars in the dark. He was about so often looking for leaks that he was called 'Night and Day'.

When Jimmy found a leak in a large main, it was all

hands to the pumps. A hole had to be dug out manually in the surface of the road and the full length of pipe exposed. Even though the water had been cut off, there would be mud and water everywhere as the men worked in the dark in the hole by the light of a hurricane lamp. Then the burst pipe was cut out and a new length put in. The joints were made watertight by hammering a length of rope coiled round the pipe into the flange to make a washer. Then the plumber would make a mould of clay round the flange, and a ladle of molten lead would be taken from the cauldron boiling on the brazier and poured into the mould to seal the joint. When all this was done and the joint had been tested under pressure and the water turned on again, the hole would be backfilled and the men would move on to wait for the rotten system to burst somewhere else in a night or two.

Walks were another thing, every Sunday after dinner with Daddy and Carmel. Down to the town hall corner to look at the old Irish milestone and decide where to go, plenty to choose from, a different route each Sunday. Sometimes out Market Street, past the station and the Market Yard, stopping to talk to old Mr Waterman, or Mr Skeffington the butcher, lamenting about the loss of trade and the disappearance of the fairs and markets which were great for Market Street, and the May Fair and the big November Fair that had spilled up the Circular Road and halfway up Irish Street, stalls everywhere, and cattle and sheep and horses and carts in every yard, and the pubs full and trade booming and now shrunk to a single day's grading a week, grading being the inspecting and classifying of animals for purchase, and Lindsay's cart selling nursery plants on a Saturday morning and not much more.

On past the Fair Green where the circuses came, Duffy's and Fawcett's and Hackenberg's, with caravans and steam engines and barred cages of wild animals, and the great marquee for the performances. There were funfairs sometimes too with roundabouts and swinging chairs and carousels and chairoplanes and music on a steam organ drawing in the crowds. The funfairs were different and more organised than the strongmen who escaped from chains, or asked men to break large stones on their chests with sledgehammers, or the snake-charmers and fire-eaters, who all came singly and performed in the streets on a winter evening, collecting money in a pouch afterwards. Past the gas-house with its sulphurous smell and the dump with a stench of rot and burning cinders, and over the Plank Drain and out past the racecourse and the stands and the horseboxes and on to the Branch Roads. Sometimes on a dry day going up a steep loaning, picking a way through the gutters, to see Magnus's grave on its hillock in the marshes. Sometimes turning back at the stone railway bridge, with its large cigarette advertisements courtesy of David Allen and Co., that bore the branch line to Killough and Ardglass, but more often braving together the lonely, bare bit of road to where it forked to Hollymount to see the gates to Ballydugan House up on one hill and the old stone toll house on the other hill which marked the old road to Dublin through Vianstown, now just a track in the fields. Or sometimes stopping short of the racecourse and turning up the other way towards the

Vianstown Road, up Grassyards Lane, where Bertie Brown's mother carried her wedding dress and her shoes down on her wedding morning and put them on at the roadside so that they would not be soiled.

Or round the Quoile. Down Church Street, past Kary Hill and Jane's Shore and round past the bridge to the floodgates. If Jack Weighman is there, going in the narrow gate past the huge old floodgate flaps now banked off and dry, across the barrier, holding on to the rail, edging and sidling along the narrow wall, one foot at a time, watching the water gushing out through the open gate below, or going out with Jack in the punt, inexpertly rowing, to take a stick out of the grille that was preventing the gate from closing, and allowing the seawater to flood in and fill the marshes and make the shops at the foot of Market Street get out their barrels and planks for walking on, and drive Bohills' cows back off the marshes and up around the Mount.

And on out round the Quoile Quay. We stop to talk to the two Mr Giffords who are laughing about the story of the man up the brae who tried to commit suicide with the butt of a fag in his mouth, and could not do so because he kept his chin above water in case the fag would go out. Or the old lady who jumped in to drown herself but was kept afloat by the air trapped in her stiff bombazine skirt, and there she was, trying vainly to get her head under the water, bobbing like an apple in a basin until somebody went out in a punt and hauled her off to the asylum. Then round to the coalyard, walking on top of the sea wall, like the battery wall in Killough, although after a bit they cheated and put pointy stones on top which you could not walk on. And yachts on the broad water, and a houseboat with a tennis court on top, which was so top-heavy it keeled over every time there was a storm and had to be righted, and the Canon's big old boat which took in water through the exhaust and sank too. Sometimes when the tide was full in, there was a regatta, with yachts and dinghies racing against each other and swimmers trying to stay upright on greasy poles, and thumping each other with feather pillows and people swimming races and diving off a spring-board fixed to the end of the coal quay and the coal-yard closed up and looking clean for a change and people in Kings Weston and the other houses at the back leaning out the top windows and waving to their friends in the crowd. Or a coal boat tied up waiting to be unloaded in the morning to slip out empty on the tide – dirty and rusting if it was English, smart and scrubbed if it were Dutch with a family living in the wheelhouse. Or if the tide was out, the mudbanks showing, only the channel clear, and sunk in the mud of either side the wooden ribs and skeletons of sunken ships.

Daddy talks to the men about the latest sensation. Two men in the town have won a fortune on the football pools, four thousand and two pounds and one penny between them. They agree that one man would keep it and the other scatter it. I wondered what they would do with the penny. Maybe split that too and take a halfpenny each. Looking into the well beside the Reverend Mr Finch-White's house who came to mass every weekday morning because there was no service in his church and shouting 'Boo! Boo!' for the echo, and running up the brae to catch up with

Daddy. Or on past the timber pond and out the Mearne Road as far as Saul church with its round tower and up the hill and down Saul Street, crossing the road to avoid passing the house where three children had been burnt to death, and crossing ourselves and saying a prayer for them. Then on, navigating by the peaks of the Mournes like sailors spotting a landmark, first the gapped top of Bearnagh, then Binnian and finally, behind the spire of the town hall, the lordly triangular shape of Donard, the highest of them all.

Or out past the war memorial with its forlorn wreaths, and the cricket ground – no play on Sundays, no play on most other days either because it was nearly always flooded – and up Harry's Loney inspecting the cattle grazing in the Farwell Fields, and on to Saul Street, and home. Or on out past the workhouse and a chat with the Master, Mr Fitzsimons, and down the Bullseye Road and back into the town that way. The Master talked about a curate who had not been happy in Downpatrick, who had not liked the people and they did not care overmuch for him. In his farewell sermon, he said that Downpatrick had been peopled from its three main public institutions. Those coming out of the gaol had been ashamed to go anywhere else, those coming out of the poorhouse had not the money for the fare, and those coming out of the asylum had not the sense to go.

Daddy was great at getting people to talk and he would hop the ball to start the game with a bit of gossip. Once he was commenting on a young man who had a name for running around with girls and said he was surprised because the boy's father was such a quiet and sober man. 'Oh, I don't know,' was the reply. 'Ould Johnny wrought a while at the weemin too.' Or the farmer who derided the ostentation involved in having wedding receptions in hotels. 'There's only room for four at a wedding – and get redd of two of them as quick as you can.'

And a man standing on the back of a lorry at an election meeting in the Shambles, with just one message. 'Don't worry boys! We'll shift this bloody border.'

Coming down the Saul Road you could see in the hollow the Bullseye Pond which supplied the water to the buildings at the top of English Street. Daddy said it was called the Bullseye because the military in Saul Camp had used it as a rifle range, but I wondered a bit about that. In the next hollow was Cochrane's Bog and a man leaning over the gate told Daddy that a young lady called Florrie Mearns, the gas manager's daughter, had been drowned there before the Great War. She had been playing hockey on the ice one winter and had fallen in. He described the efforts to save her, and men carrying her body down the street on a gate, a stern warning to everybody not to skate on thin ice, or on any ice at all.

Or up over Irish Street and Stream Street and out the Vianstown Road past the creamery, or up the hill past the planting, a small wood, to the cemetery and past the bad corner at Kellys' where all the cars crashed, and talking to Mr Kelly who Daddy said had been a great athlete, a runner, along with his brothers who won countless races for money in the north of England when they were young men bringing over cattle and sheep to sell. Mr Kelly didn't move very fast now, but he was tall and thin and spare and you could see that he might have been a runner. He reminded me of another friend that Daddy used to meet when he went to Waterford. He was a man called Peter O'Connor, who had won the long jump at the Olympic Games in Athens and had climbed up the pole afterwards to replace the Union Jack with a green flag, although he was on the British team. We all thought he was a hero, and he still held the long jump record. Daddy and Mr Kelly talked about football, about Jimmy Connor, old Johnston Connor's brother, the greatest of them all, a centre half for Belfast Celtic and Ireland. He used to drink the money they sent him for the train fare, then walk to Belfast on a Saturday morning and play the match. Still, it got him in the end. Swept away in the 1918 flu. Like snow off a ditch.

Out to the Flying Horse and round the back, past the asylum cemetery with its lych gate, to the Ardglass road and home. And on every road Daddy would meet someone he knew and stop to talk while we sat on the ditch and pretended not to listen. Sometimes it was business, sometimes weather, more times gossip, and often stories, stories, stories. Stories endlessly about Father Rhodes, who was knocked down by a tram in Belfast at Carlisle Circus and brought to the Mater Hospital. When a nurse asked him if he had brought his pyjamas, he snapped back, 'Of course I did. Of course I did. I came out to be knocked down.' Or driving his car over the footpath and through the plate glass window of a car showroom and greeting everybody cheerily, 'I was coming in anyhow.'

Daddy talking politics with a little man who had been engaged in a brief guerrilla action on the Griddle

Mountain during the Troubles. 'You know, only for the Treaty, I never would have left the army. I had a genius for soldiering.' And talk of his time in Dundalk Gaol and Ballykinlar Camp and the *Argenta*, and the Black and Tans and the terrible times they were, and thank God they can never come again, no matter what. Chamberlain's a great man. He's kept us out of the war again. If it had been Churchill we'd have been right in it. And he's sorted out the Treaty ports. Handed them back to de Valera, a sure sign that there's not going to be a war. If there had been any danger, the British would never have let them go. Much too canny for that. And he's almost fixed up the Spanish mess. After a bit of time he'll get round to dealing with partition too.

Daddy sometimes met an old comrade in arms who had served in Mesopotamia too who would greet him in mock Arabic and talk of bazaars and camels and Allenby and Jerusalem and Lawrence of Arabia and how the Arabs were let down. As we went on our way, Daddy would tell us the real story of the man stealing supplies and selling them in the bazaar and blaming it all on an Arab driver who was then punished. There was a stern warning not to take every smiling face as honest and friendly, to look behind the mask and to judge people by their actions and how they treated other people, especially those poorer than themselves.

There were another couple of old soldiers who talked about the Somme and the horror of the trenches and how lucky Daddy was not to be there, and how fortunate for them to get out of it alive. No wonder the French did not want to fight again, but to sit behind the Maginot line after all they lost in the last war. What a lot of stupid generals. Staff officers safe at the rear sending men to their deaths like cattle. Lions led by donkeys, that's what they were. At least they got back, although thousands didn't.

And then back home. Mammy still fearful of a war and conscription, and Auntie Lil too. Remembering the boy coming up the street on his bicycle with a handful of yellow envelopes. Telegrams always bringing the worst news. And Auntie Lil's husband torpedoed or mined or whatever in Lough Swilly and please God it will never come to that again.

Auntie Lil said the English were always very warlike with other people's lives. Their wars had been fought for them by the Irish and the Scots with a few Welsh thrown in. The Irish and Scots had built up the Empire for them and the English got all the plum jobs. Look at the last war – the Ulster Division wiped out in a morning on the Somme. She remembered the telegrams coming then like autumn leaves and the weeping and the wailing. And the Dublin Fusiliers on another day. And Gallipoli (which was Churchill's madness), the Irish and the Anzacs slaughtered like cattle. She began to hum an old music-hall tune and Daddy joined in the chorus:

> We don't want to fight
> But, by jingo, if we do,
> We won't go to the front ourselves
> We'll send the old Hindoo.

FOURTEEN

1 SEPTEMBER 1939, TWO YEARS TO THE DAY SINCE we had moved to Downpatrick. Earlier on that Friday, Hitler had invaded Poland and ultimatums were being given all round. It was quite clear there was going to be a war and we were all down on our knees again hoping that Hitler would turn back or Chamberlain would do the trick again. Daddy said it would be a different war this time and it would not be fought in the trenches but in the cities which would be bombed to bits. Look at Spain. We wondered where the safest place in the house would be. I crept into the little cubbyhole under the stairs and started putting down cardboard on bare timbers and pieces of carpet in case of emergency. The trouble was that the cubbyhole could not hold us all. And then there was the danger of poison gas – look at Abyssinia, Daddy said – from which we had no protection at all. Everything was in suspension until eleven o'clock on the Sunday morning, 3 September, when Mr Chamberlain would speak on the wireless. Maybe, we said, maybe after

rosaries and prayers by the dozen and innumerable visits to the chapel to fend off the evil day, and special invocations after mass on Sunday, there might be the hope that Chamberlain would come back as from Munich and say that war had been averted. But the news was of the German panzers sweeping across Poland and the Poles fighting with cavalry against tanks, and the total, overwhelming superiority of the Germans. Which led to another flicker of hope in my mother's breast that it would be all over by Sunday, the Poles would have caved in, it would be too late for the British to intervene, and we could all get back to business.

On Sunday morning, after 8.30 mass, Carmel and I went for a walk with Daddy who wanted to pass the time until the broadcast. It was a beautiful sunny day and we walked up Saul Street and on to the golf course. Up to the first green at the top of a steep hill with the whole of County Down laid out before you, smooth hills, Mourne Mountains, Strangford Lough and the Quoile in all the sharpness of a bright autumn day. We came to see the diorama that old Mr Perceval from Kary Hill had made, in a flat box on top of a square stake near the first green where the view was best. You slid back two brass fasteners and lifted the painted wooden lid and there under a pane of glass was a chart showing what you could see from there. There was a blob in the centre just above the lock with lines radiating from it like the protractor in a school geometry set, each leading to a watercolour represen-tation of what you should see if you looked in that direction. The morning was so clear, the sunshine so bright and crisp, that you could see the Mull of

Kintyre far away on the horizon where Mr Perceval said it might be. Mr Perceval was a retired Indian magistrate and his beautiful watercolours of the Quoile at Jane's Shore hung in the clubhouse. Then down, running with the slope, to the bottom, stopping, waiting for Daddy to catch up. There sitting on a bench on the first tee, looking very grumpy, was old Mr Crichton, the editor of the *Down Recorder* and a very keen golfer.

'Things are looking bad,' he said in a strong Scots accent.

'Yes indeed,' Daddy said. 'It looks like war.'

'Oh, I don't mean that. If we don't get rain soon, the greens will be ruined.'

At eleven o'clock we heard the worst in Chamberlain's flat, toneless voice: '. . . No such undertaking has been received and consequently this country is now at war with Germany.' We were soon on our knees again praying that we would all survive the war and that Daddy and Ray, now twenty-two, would not be taken. In the afternoon we listened on the spluttering radio to the All-Ireland Hurling final between Cork and Kilkenny which was interrupted by thunder and lightning; that seemed to suit the mood of the moment. That night the air-raid siren went for the first time in earnest, with its long, mournful wailing note of warning, up and down, up and down, causing us all to be roused out of bed and to rush downstairs in the dark to huddle in the kitchen under the big deal table praying, while Daddy put on his helmet and took his flash-lamp and hurried out to his office and to his post as head of the town's ARP, the Air Raid Precautions service. After an hour the siren went off again to give the all–clear in a long monotonous whine, which was a relief to hear all the same. Daddy came in soon after and said it had been a false alarm. We heard on the wireless that a passenger ship called *Athenia* had been torpedoed off the coast of Scotland and this seemed to make the war real. Aunt Lil started to talk about boats called the *Leinster* and the *Lusitania* which had been torpedoed, but she never mentioned the *Laurentic* and as usual I did not like to ask her about it.

On the previous Friday, the day Hitler invaded Poland, the order for a blackout had been imposed. This was intended to guard against air raids, to prevent towns being visible from the sky at night, and to avoid lights being used for navigation by German bombers. First of all the street lights were dowsed, making it very difficult to see in the dark. Later a few lights were permitted, fitted with masks that allowed a few weak rays to shine downwards, and the edges of the pavements and the kerbstones were painted white to make them visible. And the use of car headlamps was banned unless they were fitted with tin masks; these each had a couple of slits that allowed only a small amount of light, tilted in a downward direction, which lit up the road only a few yards ahead of the car and restricted speed to a few miles an hour. In houses it was an offence to show any light at all at night. This meant that we had to cover every window with black blinds, and mask skylights and erect complicated double screens of curtains at each outside door so that the door could be opened and closed again to let somebody in or out without allowing any stray ray of light from within the house to show. It also meant painting bulbs in the hall blue; this made the light less bright but it also meant that everybody went around with a ghastly, ghostly colouring. There were policemen and air-raid wardens doing nothing else but going around all night to see if anybody showed even a slit of light and prosecuting them. The same day the blackout was announced, there was a rush on the shops for black curtaining material and Mr Irvine and Frankie Fitzsimons were sold out, and Mammy had to go to Joe Rea, whom she did not really like, and Latimers' and even to Coburns' who had just opened up, as we scoured the town to cover all the windows in the hotel. At first we thought the wooden folding shutters would be good enough but on the first night they were seen to let out slits of light from the splits, the folds and the sides, which made the hotel blaze like a beacon in the moonless night and brought the police rushing round. Mammy made a secondary set of black curtains, whirring away on her sewing machine, and heavy cloths for draping inside the shutters, and black cloths which had to be pinned to the window frames before the shutters were closed. The skylights in the billiard room were a particular problem and the room could not be used at night until we had worked out a system of sliding blinds.

Soon soldiers came. The old gaol was opened up and could no longer be played in. One day, going up the Mall, we found the wooden gate was lying wide open, but attempts to enter the playground were rebuffed with shouts of anger; even the old German gun was out of bounds. In the afternoon, groups of men in khaki with packs on their backs and rifles on their shoulders marched three abreast up English Street from the station, the tramp of their feet causing the bottles to rattle on the bar shelves; they cut off the light from the side window of the bar which was sunk level with the footpath. The people came down from Bridge Street to stand at the corner and stare at them passing, and there was a faint cheer. They all had a strange sort of black tab attached to the collar of their battledress and hanging down the back. Ray said it was called a flash and it showed they were Welsh Fusiliers (only you spelt it with a *c*). And Joan said it had been to prevent their pigtails in the old days from staining the back of their uniform jackets when they wore red coats. On the Saturday night, as I lay in bed in the room with Ray, there was an outburst of raucous singing as drunken soldiers staggered back to barracks from the pubs. Ray, who was a romantic about these things, woke me and said, 'The Welsh. Beautiful singers. It's traditional: all those chapels and miners' choirs and rugby matches.'

There were soon all kinds of arrangements for entertaining the troops. The town hall was taken over as a sort of canteen and recreation centre. Soldiers and officers were involved in various activities around the place. Two of them were drowned trying to sail a boat in bad weather from Strangford to Newcastle, lost in the Routin' Wheel. Madness, Daddy said. They should have known better than to go out on their own and somebody should have stopped them. Nobody but a local could begin to understand the tides and shoals and rocks and currents of that coast.

Another pair of officers, drinking in the bar, met the local poacher who promised them a good day's fishing on the Rann. They thought he was an eccentric Irish landlord, filthy rich, living in a dilapidated house on a large estate, who dressed carelessly in tattered trousers and a ragged jacket and didn't bother to wash himself or to shave too well either. They were getting very excited about the prospect of a day's sport when he said to them, 'I suppose you'll be able to square the bloody peelers?'

It was not all sweetness. Some of the boys in school used to boast of turning the signposts at crossroads through ninety or a hundred and eighty degrees in order to put soldiers astray and to send convoys of tanks and guns and lorries and half-tracks and armoured cars miles out of their way on country roads.

As I was going up Saul Street to school one morning, walking briskly to keep pace with a friend on a bicycle, I was startled by the roar of two motorbikes bearing army despatch riders, flashing up the road with messages for General Pollock up at Rathkeltair House. My friend was startled too as he turned slowly across the road into the school gate. Unfortunately there was a third motorcyclist some distance behind the other two and he ploughed into the bike, threw the rider into the air and then crashed into the wall beside the well, finishing up bleeding and senseless on the ground. My friend had a broken leg and was badly shaken up. The soldier had a broken skull and brain damage and never left the mental hospital after.

One evening there was a friendly soccer match in the Down High School grounds between a scratch Downpatrick side and a team of soldiers. Ray was playing for Downpatrick. As I stood on the concrete path, I heard a woman say to her ageing boyfriend, 'What does he think of himself, playing soccer with a lot of Protestants against the army?' I could sense that there were three different sins there, but I could not be sure which one was the worst.

FIFTEEN

THE WAR WAS A GREAT GEOGRAPHY LESSON IN the old borders of Europe and North Africa. The papers were full of maps and diagrams showing the German lines and the Allied lines and arrows tracing how the panzers had blitzkrieged across Europe and beyond. A lone whistler going home up Bridge Street every night whistled 'Tantum Ergo' which was really 'Deutschland über Alles', the German national anthem in disguise, just to annoy the B Specials who were stopping people in the blackout at Breens' corner. Old Albert Coulter, the commandant, made a fool of himself jumping out in front of cars and making people give their names whom he knew quite well, and creeping round to test the defences at General Pollock's house at Rathkeltair and nearly getting himself shot by the army. Everybody laughed about it. He was a decent enough man in the daytime when he was a solicitor's clerk in the offices across the road, a bit severe when you met him on the footpath in Saul Street in the morning going to school, but civil enough to return a salute. He got a bit distant when the flags were out coming up to the marching season, but so did they all, or going up English Street on a Sunday, bowler-hatted with a rolled umbrella and Bible and prayerbook in hand to play the organ at the cathedral. At night in B Special uniform he was Lucifer jumping out from the shadows to challenge the world. Daddy said he was all right: no harm in him really. It was just that after being ordered about all day, when he got into uniform and had a couple of men under him the sense of power went to his head.

During the phoney war, which lasted from the declaration of war till May 1940, nothing happened to the Maginot line or the Siegfried line although the radio kept blaring out, 'We will hang out the washing on the Siegfried line if the Siegfried line's still there.' We gathered at night, furtively, behind drawn curtains and closed doors to listen to Lord Haw-Haw: 'Germany calling, Germany calling, Hamburg, Bremen and Dortmund, on the medium waveband.' There were all sorts of topical references you were never lucky enough to hear in the static, but which boys at school could talk about next day: that the town hall clock in Downpatrick was twenty minutes slow, or that people in Killough were starving for want of an egg. Daddy's story was that old Kitty McSherry was so annoyed that she held the frying pan up to the loudspeaker and challenged Haw-Haw to smell that.

Then there was the German strike into Norway, and lessons about iron ore and supply routes, and into Denmark and through the Netherlands and Belgium,

and would the French stop them at the Marne this
time? And people straggling home from Dunkirk with
news of others who would never come back. Poor
Billy Nolan whose lorry moved our furniture in from
Killough, now lost without trace. Daddy said that
Tommy Collins had seen him sitting on a ditch about
twelve miles from Dunkirk and maybe he was all
right. And Ray telling about Sam Corry who had been
a doctor in the infirmary getting off on the last boat
from Bordeaux and the Germans firing on them from
the banks as they sailed up the long river to the sea,
which I didn't believe for a moment – it wasn't the sort
of thing you could have done on the Quoile. And our
own fear of invasion: the church bells stopped ringing
and while the war lasted would only be rung again if
the Germans came. And there were Home Guards and
Local Defence Volunteers and only Protestants allowed to join, and more and more B Specials. And
more distrust even than before of the B Specials, because in the blackout they would stand at Breens'
corner and frighten the wits out of people by jumping
up with guns and shouting 'Halt!' And stopping cars
whose drivers could scarcely see the road because only
a thin slit of light could pass through the masks on the
headlamps, and moreover only stopping them at the
last minute so that the drivers nearly crashed into them
and got told off for that too. And there were more
worries about conscription and all the Protestants had
got themselves into the Home Guard and into reserved
occupations so that only Catholics would be taken, and
if they were so keen on the war they could join up anyhow and not wait to be pressed, sitting up there in their
safe jobs in the courthouse, full of loyalty when it suited

them. Maybe de Valera would stop it. Daddy said he wouldn't depend on him for a moment. Maybe the cardinal would do it, or the pope, or better still say our prayers and ask for God's help.

The war was good for business. The hotel filled up with officers' wives and there was a full dining room for dinner every night and James Blaney was in his element rushing up and down stairs with orders, his white moustache bristling and his swallowtails flying behind him. As well as soldiers there were the people who were in on big construction contracts for army camps and aerodromes which were being built everywhere. Cryers and Carmichaels were building an airfield at Bishopscourt and their executives visited regularly, the site engineers stayed permanently, and there was a constant stream of lorries full of men, many from the South, who lodged all over the town and were employed as tradesmen. The queues at the Buroo shortened as men were taken on in contracts or were sent to England to work under threat of being struck off as unwilling to work. Daddy said there were fortunes being made by quarrymen who supplied stone to the contractors and who kept driving a lorryload of stone in through one gate and out through another at the other side without unloading it, but getting paid all the time.

George Pile was one of a group of eccentrics who came to stay in the hotel during the war, along with the regular schoolteachers and bank clerks and civil servants. He was English, a small precise man, very courteous, with a white moustache, who fascinated us by giving hand signals when reversing and turning his car in the hotel yard. He was in some mysterious way associated with the aerodrome, and with some sort of secret weapon for tracking aeroplanes, or the radar station then being just on the point of emerging from secrecy and blocking off the banks of Killard from the rambler and the naturalist, the bather and the Sunday hurler. Mr Pile was not prompt about paying his bills which was why Mammy was anxious that he should never hear any hint that the recess in front of the hotel was a debtors' sanctuary. There was an article in the *Irish News* by Colin Johnston Robb telling all about it and Mammy was terrified that Mr Pile would see it and pay even more slowly than usual, and she had us going round the house hiding copies of the newspaper.

The first of the visitors from outer space had been Captain de Rouffignac who was a captain in the Welch Fusiliers and soon became a fixture in the bar. Here he was known as Rouffy. He was the RTO, the Rail Traffic Officer, and he had a small office at the station next to Mr Foster the stationmaster, where he went every day to arrange trains for soldiers. He had a little badge on his sleeve showing a bird in a nest. He said it meant the Northern Ireland District and was a pun on the French word for a nest, *un nid*. I told him the Irish for a nest was *nead*, but he did not seem to think there was any connection. Another visitor was an elderly, pompous man called Binney who was a second lieutenant, the most junior commissioned rank, when he started off, but became a captain later. He was in charge of intelligence, which seemed strange since Daddy said he was one of the few men who really were as stupid as they looked. He used to come down the stairs in broad daylight shining a flashlamp into the corners of the landings in case there was an IRA man lying in wait for him. He took the *Daily Telegraph*, the first time we had seen it, and bought exotic things in Kidds' – Gentleman's Relish (patum peperium) and Carrs' Water Biscuits. One morning he offended Mr Moore by asking for his papers in a haughty tone; and when Johnny would have none of this Binney drew himself up and asked him if he was aware that he was addressing one of His Majesty's officers. To which Johnny, who had just lost a son in the war, snarled, 'And a bloody stupid one too to be only a second lieutenant at your age.'

Binney was always on the lookout for people doing strange and suspicious things, as if he expected all the time to be blown up or shot. One day he looked out of the dining-room window and saw James Hampton, with a turnkey as tall as himself, turning off the water at a stopcock in the middle of the road at the town hall corner. Binney called James Blaney over and asked him what that man was doing. Jimmy said he was winding the town hall clock, that he did it every eighth day. That seemed to satisfy Binney.

These officers had batmen, and we found it very strange to see grown men waiting in a servile way on other men who treated them at best curtly and mostly with contempt. There were the officers' wives too, who went round talking to each other in loud voices as if you were not there. One of them went into old Mrs Hanlon to ask where she could get mistletoe for Christmas. Mrs Hanlon, from a strong republican background, replied, 'They do say there's plenty in Germany if you were to go for it.'

In the hotel it was all very hard work for everybody.

Getting supplies was an adventure as rationing became more strict: first sugar, then tea and butter and meat, until the tea and butter ration was about two ounces a week. Early in the war the abattoir was taken over by the Ministry, and all the private slaughterhouses were closed in order to control the supply of meat. There were coupons for sweets and clothes and almost everything you wanted to buy. People had to give up some coupons for meat when they had a meal in the hotel and these had to be handed in and accounted for. The fact that the hotel was there made it a lot easier for us, but it also meant a constant recourse to friends in the country for butter and eggs, and to what we afterwards discovered was called the 'black market'. This meant getting country butter, fresh and salty, and farmer's eggs, still warm, with straw and dirt sticking to them, and pork and bacon from people who killed and cured their own pigs, sometimes not very well cured so that the bacon turned out green, or getting meat from a butcher who killed surreptitiously on his premises rather than in the abattoir, afterhours when nobody was about, sometimes in the early hours of a Sunday morning. Simon Waterman, the brother of the shoe-maker, who worked in Muldrews' grocer's would always give you scarce things or a bit on the rations if he could, and there was also smuggling across the border, with meat and butter and bacon and whiskey being brought one way and sugar and tea and white flour the other. Not that the flour was all that white, and it gradually became browner and coarser as the war went on.

My aunt in Kerry who had always sent the *Kerryman* every week, mostly folded and tied with twine in a particular way so as to go through the post, now discovered that she could send a few rashers of bacon in between the pages. Which had the effect of making the paper transparent and unreadable where the lard had been absorbed, or of decorating the streaky bacon with broad black bands of newsprint. And when the post had been held up for a day or two, it caused half the dogs in the town to follow the postman on his rounds.

We went on holidays, Daddy and I, to Waterford, even during the war, and the journey became more of an odyssey than ever. You could not do it in a single day but had to spend a night in a hotel in Dublin, generally the same one where Mammy had stayed the night before she was married, near the church off the quays where the wedding took place, where we went to mass in the morning for old time's sake. To get from one station to the other there were infrequent trams or horse-drawn cabs, hansom cabs, Daddy called them, or traps or closed carriages, like at funerals, or the odd motor with a great bag of gas on the roof. Sometimes too there was not a train on the main line and we had to go round the coast on the Dublin and South Eastern Railway, the Doubly Slow and Easy, Daddy called it, along the coast to Wexford and back to Waterford that way. Sometimes the train was so low on fuel that it could scarcely get up steam. Sometimes indeed it stopped altogether and the driver and guard and some of the passengers went off to gather sticks and branches and sods of turf to burn in the fire. But Daddy was always welcome in Waterford because he brought tea which was much scarcer in the South than at home.

In the South the papers didn't talk about the war.

They called it 'the Emergency', but there were soldiers and coastguards there too. One day I cycled out to see a German plane that had crashed after being shot at over the Irish Channel. The strands and coves were full of goods washed in from torpedoed ships, and sometimes a mine floated in which would blow up beside a fishing boat.

There were lots of young people away at sea or in the British forces or working in England, just like home, but it was still not the real war: no blackouts, no tanks and troop carriers on the roads, certainly no B Specials, no uniforms in the streets, plenty of butter, bacon and meat, no coupons for sweets. The talk was mainly of rust in wheat and foot-and-mouth disease in cattle. There was no news of battles in the newspapers.

It was a sort of relief to get back to the real war.

SIXTEEN

THE GREAT EVENT OF THE WAR WAS THE BLITZ on Belfast. There were often air-raid warnings, the siren mounted on the roof of the police barracks wailing out a lonely message of warning, rising and falling. If it was at night, we all got up and crept downstairs to the kitchen with blankets, careful not to show a light, and sat under the strong deal table. Daddy, who now had a green helmet with white letters on it saying ARP CONTROLLER, rushed out to the office in the dark. As he went out Auntie Lil threw holy water after him and Mammy said prayers and then we all said the rosary that he would come back safely and there would be no bombs and the house would not be wrecked and we would all survive. Sometimes you would hear an aeroplane and you could tell the German ones because they made more of a drone and sounded very menacing as they approached and went away again, and if you went out into the yard you could see searchlights outside Belfast like giant lighthouse beams probing the sky in great arcs, intersecting and switching off again. Oddly enough, you rarely heard a British aeroplane at night, although you would recognise the sound of Hurricanes and Spitfires in the daytime. After an hour or two the siren would blow again, the relieving note of the all-clear. Mammy and Auntie Lil would make us say the rosary again, and then you could go off to bed for what remained of the night.

The air-raid precautions started to be visible. The fire brigade got a proper pump on a trailer with a second-hand car to pull it, and a couple of large old cars were cut down and converted to ambulances with angle-iron racks in the back to carry stretchers. Public air-raid shelters were built in the streets which took up the whole footpath and were a hazard in the blackout. Worse still, nobody would go into them because they became temporary public lavatories for people who were short-taken so that the smell was enough to drive away even the most lustful courting couples who resorted there for privacy in the evenings. There were fears too, voiced by the experts at the street corners, that the brick construction would not stand up to blast because the contractor had a bad name for shoddy workmanship and for skimping on cement. All in all, it was thought that you were much safer outside them; most people stayed in the house, following the advice of the leaflets to bunk down under the stairs or to get under a large table until the all-clear.

The clear moonlit nights were worst because that was when the planes came and the warnings were more frequent. There was a story in one of my school-books of an old Irish monk in his monastery copying out scriptures and scribbling in the margin a little prayer that the seas would be rough in the night and the tempests high with ice and snow because then the Vikings would be less likely to attack.

> Tonight the wind is strong
> The sea is wild,
> I do not fear the hordes of hell
> Coming up the Irish Channel

Sitting under the kitchen table trying to read by candlelight, I often felt like that monk, praying for a stormy, rainy, cloudy night, when the moon was covered and German planes could not fly.

One bright moonlit night the all-clear did not go and instead of a single plane there seemed to be dozens. Ray went out to the yard and said you could see them flying over in threes, right across the town, right up over Bridge Street and on towards Belfast. And the glass in the windows shook and you could feel the menace in the air as if the house was going to fall in on its own before anybody dropped a bomb on it or shot it up. Soon you could hear the crump and thump of explosions in Belfast and see flashes of light and then sustained flames on the skyline as the fires took hold.

There was an all-clear in the grey dawn but Daddy came home for his breakfast and a shave looking very tired. He said there had been a big raid on Belfast and hundreds of people were killed and Jack Weighman and the fire brigade had gone off to Belfast to help put out the fires. Later there was news on the wireless that the Dundalk, Drogheda, Dublin and Dún Laoghaire fire brigades had gone too, had driven straight there through the night. Daddy said de Valera must have sent them without being asked, for

Dawson Bates would never have brought himself to ask for help from the South even if there was not a fireman left in Belfast and the whole place was torching. He said MacDermott was a good man who had tried to do something about air-raid precautions but Dawson Bates was a stupid old bigot who was corrupt into the bargain. Mammy was crying for Claire who had just started working in a hospital in Belfast, and we said some more prayers for her.

I had joined the APR as a messenger since this was the only means of getting a torch and batteries with which to read in bed, and a belt and a tin hat, and maybe after a bit a better class of gas mask, and a silver badge to wear in your buttonhole. It said ARP and had a crown over it and Mammy said I was not to wear it in school because it would annoy the Brothers and might even cause rows with the other boys.

Now I was called into service. Early in the war, everybody had been issued with a gas mask in a little cardboard box with a string to carry it over your shoulder which everybody was supposed to take everywhere with them, but which, after a week or two, very few people did, as if they would only be gassed at home. The gas mask was an ugly rubber face mask with a celluloid panel to see out through and a snout formed from a perforated canister which contained the filter to purify the gas. The mask was smelly and clammy and very unpleasant to wear, and you were only supposed to put it on after a special warning given by gas wardens waving wooden rattles which made a noise like corncrakes. Then, after a bit, it was discovered that the Germans had a new gas which the gas mask would not protect you from and everybody had to take their masks into a centre to get a new extra filter fitted. This was about the size of a large tin of shoe polish and had to be lined up with the edges of the existing filter and secured by a couple of rounds of sticky tape. The nuns in the convent had not bothered to have their gas masks adapted and when the bombs came they sent down to the council office in a panic for somebody to fit the new filters at once. Since everybody else was very busy, I was sent up to the convent with a couple of boxes of filters and a couple of rolls of white sticky tape and powdered chalk to shake on them to take away the stickiness, and a big new pair of scissors.

At the convent I was brought into the parlour just inside the door and installed in state. The nuns came in in pairs with their gas masks in their little cardboard boxes which had never been opened, the masks inside untried and the webbing straps unattached and unadjusted. As I fixed them, the nuns were in a hunger for news, especially those who came from Belfast, and wanted to know what was going on in the outside world and whether their families were safe. They kept asking me about areas of Belfast I had never heard of and whether there had been bombs there – which I did not know any more than they did. But if they looked kind or I liked them or they were not bossy like some of the nuns, I told them there were no bombs in that particular district and that their relatives were probably safe enough and would get in touch with them as soon as the phones had been fixed. But when the nun who had once pinned paper round Helen's dress and been cruel to Carmel asked whether her brother's business had been bombed, I said it almost certainly had, even though I didn't have a clue. In fact the business had been badly damaged.

Back in the council office just before lunch time I saw crowds of people straggle up Irish Street from the train, mothers pushing prams with bundles of clothes stacked on top of the babies and rickety Tansads, and dragging crying and screaming children behind them and all looking dirty and unkempt and unslept and miserable. As they came up past the Cup and Saucer and up the laundry steps, Daddy said they were evacuees from Belfast, getting out before the night came again and another raid, and there would be trainloads more coming in during the rest of the day. He had commandeered all the schools and halls and had people filling large sacks called palliasses with straw from the hotel yard or Bohills' or Menowns' and laying them out on the floor for people to sleep on. We went up to the Green High to see some of the people settled in and bedded down for the night. When we came home for something to eat, Mammy made us stand on newspapers on the tiled floor in front of the kitchen fire while she shook shoals of fleas and nits out of our clothes and killed them on the floor. Still we were not allowed upstairs, but had to stand in a tin bath on the floor and be sluiced down with Jeyes fluid and washed with carbolic soap while our clothes were rushed off into a tub of bleach to steep. Then Mammy got going with a fine-tooth comb and a sheet of white paper, combing the nits and lice out of our hair and cracking them with her thumbnail against the back of the comb, leaving little splotches of blood on her nail and a black mark on the paper. This ritual was to be repeated nightly during the chaotic days that followed.

Back with the evacuees next morning, I had never seen dirt or filth or degradation like it. The smell was awful, made worse by babies dirtying their nappies and having to be changed, or running around naked from the waist down, with faeces dripping down their legs, and leaving the imprint of tiny feet on the floor. There was a stench of decay, and almost of despair as the poor people cried for members of their families they had lost or could not find or their husbands who were still in Belfast, or their little houses which had been destroyed or blown down or burnt, or which would be looted or despoiled before they got back because they had run out in what they stood up in, some in nightclothes, and had not waited to lock the door.

Daddy said some of the smell was caused by fear, but most by the squalor of the wretched houses they lived in, and it was a disgrace to humanity to expect people to live like animals – in worse accommodation than horses and cows – and he hoped whoever won the war this time they would do something about it or people would rise up and you couldn't blame them.

During all the next day the trains kept coming in, the people frightened and tense and exhausted after having spent the night in the open in the fields around Belfast. They were shocked by the suddenness of the attack, which they had believed would never happen because Belfast was so far away for the planes to come, by the lack of anti-aircraft protection, and by the chaos and lack of direction and the destruction in the city. The attack disrupted life in Downpatrick too, as people landed in on relatives or knocked on the doors of strangers asking to be taken in. There was a little man who looked after the council dump on the

Ballydugan Road just across the road from the railway station. He could not read the clock or tell the time, so the normal routine was that his mother sent him out to work in the morning, and he knew that the third train coming across the marshes was the twelve o'clock arrival from Ardglass and it was time to go home for lunch. She sent him out again, and then, three trains later, the six o'clock from Newcastle and it was time to go home. Now, with trains arriving every hour, his system of timekeeping was destroyed and he arrived home for lunch before half past nine, and knocked off for the day at about three o'clock. He was so confused that he went home without damping down the incinerator; it blazed up in the night, causing great alarm in the blackout in case it would bring the bombers back, and to Downpatrick this time.

The evacuees were fed from the school meals kitchens and were then moved to outlying schools and halls in order to relieve the pressure as more and more trains arrived from Belfast. Milk had to be delivered in cans, and tinned food was requisitioned from local shops with special ration coupons and delivered round. This was a job I got along with Derek King who drove the Armstrong Siddeley ambulance as an ARP volunteer. I was taken because I knew the back roads from travelling around with Bertie Small the tillage officer who stayed in the hotel and often took me out for company. Since all the signposts had been removed in case of invasion, he would throw me a map and tell me to find the way to the farms he was visiting that day to see that they had ploughed all the land they were supposed to have broken up, and what they had put in it, and whether it was seven-year lea, grassland that had not been ploughed for at least seven years and was therefore eligible for subsidy, or something else. This gave me a great knowledge of the countryside and the roads and farms and townland names, which were like poetry – Ballymacaramery, Lisoid, Tullymacnous, Magheracranmoney, Inch, Killinchy-in-the-Woods, Florida, Jericho, Bright, Aughlisnafin, Ballytrim and Ballysallagh, Carrowbaghran and Spittle Ballee.

This was very useful knowledge to have, so I was attached to Derek as his navigator and we began to transport evacuees, billeting them in private houses where there was room, or in empty houses and sometimes in farm buildings. We would go out with a vanload of people and a list of houses to put them in. Most of the evacuees were from a Catholic area of Belfast, but not all, and most of the houses with room to spare belonged to Protestants, but nearly all were very welcoming and never raised a question. Once or twice when somebody asked what religion the evacuees were before they would agree to take them, we said we did not know, and picked out the largest, most troublesome family with the most children, dirty and festooned with holy pictures pinned on to their jerseys and scapulars and rosary beads just to teach the farmer and his wife a lesson in tolerance. Most of the evacuees were grateful just for the shelter, but some were hard to please and some the house owners could not put up with and we had to shift them elsewhere. One family was shifted five or six times; strangely enough, having started with few possessions they seemed to have more and more every time we moved them.

After a week or so, with the worst of the panic over, the schools reopened after the holidays. There was another air raid on Belfast about a month later, but this time it was mainly with incendiary bombs, and since the people had mostly cleared out or taken to the hills for the night, there were fewer human casualties. By then our evacuees had moved to permanent billets or to rent houses for themselves or to lodge with families. Some of them stayed in the Downpatrick area for the rest of the war and some for ever.

Later, Jack Weighman told me his adventures with the fire brigade in Belfast. When they arrived, there seemed to be nobody in charge, and there were fallen and burning buildings everywhere and great holes in the ground and an air-raid shelter full of people blown up with hundreds of bodies being taken out and laid in drained-out swimming pools to be identified. Worst of all for a fire brigade, there was no water, because all the water mains had been blown up. So Jack and his crew had dismounted the pump from the trailer and taken it down to the river at the Short Strand and followed the water out across the glar as the tide went out until they had run out of hose and could do no more. After a couple of days in which they had had very little food and still nobody to tell them what to do, and with the fires at last burning themselves out, they had come home and gone to bed.

And still no news of poor Billy Nolan.

SEVENTEEN

ONE DAY, WHEN THE WAR HAD BEEN GOING for a good while, Mammy's nephew Moss, my namesake, appeared out of the blue. He had been rather lost sight of, working in England for years, and despite his flat feet and general unfitness he had been conscripted into the army. Thinking that it would be nice to join an Irish regiment, he had picked the Ulster Rifles, which was largely Protestant and from the North, rather than the Royal Irish Fusiliers, which was mainly Dublin and Catholic. It didn't seem to make much difference, and he got a soft job for a while going to Belfast from the depot in Ballymena each day as a helper on a lorry collecting supplies. It seemed to be easy for him to disappear for the day and come down to Downpatrick on the bus for a feed and a rest. He used to take me on long walks to get him out of the house and from under Mammy's feet. I was attached by Auntie Lil as a brake to discourage him from going into pubs on the way and getting drunk, which he never showed any inclination to do.

He was seen around the town and one of my classmates referred to him rather disdainfully as 'your
Swaddy' (a corruption, I supposed, of *squaddie*) as if it
were not a respectable thing to have a close relative in
the army, even as a conscript. Moss was soon transferred to England; he wrote to me long letters from
Yeovil and other towns in the South of England as
the army prepared for the invasion of Europe. However, his flat feet and fallen arches were too much even
for the Ulster Rifles, and he was discharged to do war
work in factories in England.

One Sunday evening when Cousin Moss was visiting, there was an announcement on the radio that the
Japanese had bombed the American fleet in a place
called Pearl Harbor, which we had never heard of, in
a place called Honolulu which we had, just, from the
pictures. Daddy said that was the end of it, the Americans would come into the war with too much money,
too many men, too much industry and power, and in
the end they would win.

Shortly afterwards the Americans arrived in Belfast
and the Yanks began to be seen around. They were
better-dressed and had more money than the British
soldiers, and they looked fitter and more healthy too.
Soon their huge tanks were trundling around; although as they ran on rubber tracks they made less
noise than the smaller British ones, their size as they
lumbered up English Street made the bottles shake in
the presses in the boxroom.

The Americans brought a whole new range of experience. They were prolific spenders – they would
give any money for drink especially for a quart of
whiskey as they called a ten-glass bottle – and they

were good customers for the hotel. They created a demand for T-bone steaks – nobody knew what they were until Mammy worked out that it was a rib steak with the bone and the fillet left in, and got that cut from the butchers, and then they got plenty of them. They tipped very well too, much to the delight of James Blaney who preferred them to the English. One cross English officer who could not get a steak one night asked sharply what were the qualifications to eat a steak in the hotel. James replied gruffly, 'Good teeth, sir!'

The bar was very busy, particularly at night. Closing time was nine o'clock, but that only meant closing the front door, making sure the blackout was perfect and there was no glimmer of light showing through a crack, closing over the shutters to make sure, and carrying on with the business. Regular customers had a sort of special knock which they used on the brass knocker on the front door. Others could ring the bell and negotiate; if they looked to be civil, they would be let in. The lounges would be full too, and at weekends the back room and upstairs. One night the conversation was so loud that Constable Tommy Donaldson, on duty in English Street, put his head round the door and told them to keep quiet: 'For all you know there could be a policeman outside.' The trouble was that sometimes Tail-light came and then everybody had to rush down the yard and out the back gate.

The Yanks brought delights we had never heard of: tinned salted peanuts, Hershey bars, guava jelly, Spam luncheon meat. A man from Valentia Island, in Kerry, arrived to open a Western Union office in the café where old Mr Borza had made his ice cream, now renamed the Mo-ee. From here they sent their cables home. They badly upset the sexual balance in the town, being very popular with the girls whom they brought out in lorryloads to dances in the camps. Girls who went were regarded as being not very respectable, for the American approach to courtship was both more direct and more public than anything we had been used to. Some people said that there would be so many American babies about that next time they would just send the uniforms over.

In many ways the Americans were simple boys far from home. One girl would get her Yank to leave her home to the convent door, the convent being the biggest building in Irish Street, pretending that it was her house and that her father would be mad if he found them there in the blackout when the door was opened. And one night, late, the Canon was picking his way down the Folly Lane by flashlight on his way home in the dark. He came upon a Yank heavily engaged with a girl in the lee of an electric-light pole. He said, very crossly, 'Isn't it time you pair were in bed?' To which the GI cheekily retorted, 'Gee, honey, there's a lot in what the old guy says!'

Some houses which soldiers frequented got a bad name, we were not very sure for what, nothing specific said but much nodding and sniffing and raising of eyebrows and if you only knew, missus, all I could tell you about that. There was one house in Saul Street that people talked about in this way as a 'bad house'. One morning, as I went up to school on my own, an old lady came out of the door with a raincoat over her nightdress and no stockings and her feet pushed into men's boots as she shuffled out to the step. I was on the other side of the road, behind the little wall where the footpath ran beneath the level of the street, and she called me over. She had a letter in her hand which she wanted me to read for her. I went up the little steps and across the road to the other footpath. I looked at her and I looked in through the open door where her daughters were lying about in their shifts. I saw the Brothers coming up the street and crowds of boys passing on the other side and staring across and I took to my heels and ran. I have never been so ashamed of anything and I think of that poor woman, having got a letter in the post which she was not able to read from her soldier son who was lost in Greece or Crete or somewhere and who was looking for help which I denied to her from a false sense of respectability, or in case someone would chastise me, or for fear of mockery, or because of the unnamed sinfulness that I had been led to associate with the place, and I let her down. I can still see her turning to go back in through the door, with the letter crumpled in her hand and her head bowed and her feet shuffling along in the old boots.

For the first time too, the Yanks brought us into contact with colour prejudice. There was only one family of black people in Downpatrick, who lived in Bridge Street and as it happened shared our surname. Daddy said there were three kinds of Hayes in Downpatrick: one were black Protestants, the others were Protestant blacks, and us. We knew old Sarah well because she sat on her seat outside the door on a sunny day. She had two children, both grown up, Olive and Jimmy. But they were part of the furniture in Bridge Street and nobody paid any attention to their colour. It was a great shock then to see black soldiers having to step off the pavement when white soldiers walked down it, and not being allowed to go into bars where white Americans drank – which meant nearly every bar in the town. And yet they were quiet and polite and there was great sympathy for them and lots of stories about how much decenter they were and better-behaved than the other Yanks.

Our ideas of the USA had been formed from the pictures which offered images of sophistication and wealth. They did not prepare us for the farm boys from the Midwest who were landed on our streets saying 'Ma'am' to all the women. It was a surprise to find out that some of them had never been in a city, that they did not know Chicago or New York or James Cagney or Edward G. Robinson or the Dead End Kids or the Three Stooges and that the first time they had seen the sea was when they were put on a boat and sailed at great speed across the Atlantic.

The presence of the Yanks all added to the pressure to deal and barter, to get supplies and to dodge the controls. Out to the country on a bicycle for eggs and butter, dodging round back ways for beef from the butchers, travelling back in the blackout, stopping to hear if the person in front was challenged by a police patrol, cutting back through the church graveyard, past the grave of Russell in the dark, up the steps to Bridge Street and down home to avoid the patrol at the post office. And the odd foray to Dublin or Dundalk on the train and the anguish at Goraghwood as roasts of beef were concealed beneath the seat and raincoats spread as the customs men made their way down the train, the wondering if the other passengers were friendly or spies, and the sight of old women made obese by the contraband hidden in their clothes, and the people who smuggled sausages or silk stockings by wrapping them round their waists or dropping them down trouser legs, and all the time the hunt for points and coupons and permits to allow the trade to go on.

Meantime the geography lessons went on as the Germans swept across Russia and the Ukraine, up to Leningrad, which our books called St Petersburg, and across to the Crimea where Errol Flynn, whose father had a house at Kilclief, had ridden so heroically and so hopelessly in *The Charge of the Light Brigade*. All the old names were there, like Balaclava and Sevastopol, where Florence Nightingale had been the Lady with the Lamp, although Auntie Lil said it was a few Irish Sisters of Mercy from Dublin who did all the work while she got all the credit. There were maps in the papers with great arrows pointing right across to Stalingrad on the Volga, and on down to Persia, and Mesopotamia which Daddy knew all about, and through the Khyber Pass to India, and talk in history lessons about the 'great game', which was the struggle between England and Russia for control of India. There were new, unpronounceable Russian names of places and people, like Zukhov and Timoshenko. Daddy said jokingly that Timoshenko might be Irish too, and Mammy, strong in the belief that every hero was a Kerryman, every Kerryman a hero, agreed with Auntie Lil that he was probably a son of Tim O'Shea of Dromin who had run off with a Russian circus that had visited Listowel in the second year of the South African war.

I was reading *War and Peace*, a great feat of endurance, the book having been put aside for me as a regular reader by Mrs Cochrane the Carnegie Library's part-time librarian and Bertie Brown's sister; the cathedral-like rafters of the library made the whole place like a church, a bit holy, not to be talked in except by the old men reading their daily papers in the outside room, and the books too to be respected like sacramental things, to be handled carefully and not to be scuffed or written on or tea spilt on, and the pages not to be turned down at the corners to mark the place. No smell of incense and colza oil or candles burning, but the light through the high leaded windows, specks of dust dancing in the sunbeams which made a page hard to read, and a smell of must and damp, more like the cathedral than the chapel, but a holy place just the same.

Finishing *War and Peace*, read by torchlight under the blankets, was like leaving a village where you had lived for years and got to know all the people, and learning too that invading armies had been to Russia before and the Russians had just walked back and back in front of Napoleon and burned Moscow and left him to get back home in the winter, and that the frost and the snow and the hunger had killed him off without the Russians having to do very much. Maybe the same thing would happen again.

Then there was the ebb and flow of battle across North Africa and a new geography lesson on Libya and Tripoli and Egypt and the Sudan. Rommel became a popular hero and the midnight whistler added 'Lili Marlene' to his repertoire to annoy the B Specials as he walked home up Bridge Street. The Far East and

China, where all the missionaries had gone who were now being killed and starved, was where Auntie Lil's china tea set had come from. It was now locked in the glass cabinet upstairs, a treasure brought home to her long ago by her sailor husband. Singapore fell as the Japanese swooped down through Malaya where, Daddy said, the guns had been installed to point the wrong way, to face enemies from the sea and not from the jungle behind them. Mammy said that General Maxwell, who had been in charge, could not have been very good anyhow because he had been beaten by a handful of the IRA in County Cork and had surrendered his sword to Tom Barry when he was a young man. Or maybe he was just very unlucky, in which case they would have been better with someone else.

Battleships were being sunk regularly, like *Repulse* and *Prince of Wales*, and there were stories all the time of men from Killough and round the shore who had been torpedoed or lost at sea, and people who would not come back, and the fear in the place of the telegraph boy on his bicycle with his yellow envelopes. And one of Ray's schoolfriends from Killough a prisoner of war in Hong Kong. Daddy met a boy from Killough who told him he had been married in Liverpool in a hurry and he had had to get it done by the dog licence man, but he would bring her back to Killough after the war to get Father Napier to do the job right.

There were Spitfire Weeks and Warship Weeks ('Buy a squadron of destroyers from County Down!') and Weapons Weeks and Wings for Britain Weeks in rapid succession. These were government campaigns to get money to bankroll the war: to raise war loans and to sell savings certificates and bonds, or savings stamps which could be stuck on a card until you had enough for a certificate, and post-war credits, no money paid out until after the war was over. Mammy said to buy if the rate was good and not to worry – if the Germans won the war the money would be valueless anyhow like the German marks after the last war when it took a million marks to buy a pound of butter and the notes were worth less than the purse you put them in.

A big model of a barometer was mounted on the post office wall at the bottom of English Street just behind the Jubilee lamp; the barometer went up to the upstairs windows with a bulb painted silver at the bottom and, rather oddly, a red line to show the mercury going up, which was lengthened every day during the Wings for Britain Week to show how much money had been collected locally until there was enough money to buy a Spitfire: £5,000.

I used to be sent out on a bicycle for fruit and vegetables to one or other of the big houses around that had gardens and gardeners – Finnebrogue or Kary Hill or Castle Ward – a long cycle ride for gooseberries or peas or soft fruit, and worse if you had to pick them in the hot sun as well, awful as they squashed in a basket hanging from the handlebars on the way home and the juice splashed your knees and bare thighs and shins. Better to ramble round to the Mount or up the Gallows Hill or to Sampson's Stone and the Dam Hill for blackberries and to do it in your own time and eat some without having to squint around in case you were accused of thieving, and walk home with them in one of Mr Galbraith's gallon cans, and bring in the cows as well, saving a double journey.

One old lady sold flowers from her garden for the war effort, with a big sign saying it was for Mrs Churchill's Aid to Russia Fund. Mammy said it was in case anybody would think she was in trade or was doing it for the money. I used to be sent for the flowers and got long lectures on our gallant Russian allies, which I stood as long as I could because although she did not seem to have been taught about the evils of godless communism or the wickedness of the Bolsheviks, or to have read Owen Francis Dudley's books about the crucifixion of White Russians, or even *War and Peace*, Mammy needed the flowers and they were very nice and hard to get otherwise. One day I told the old lady that if the Russians won the war she would be in real trouble because they were all communists and did not like people like her, and I would be in trouble because I was a Catholic and we would both probably end up in a salt mine in Siberia, but she would be worse off than me. She would not give me the flowers and chased me away. I was not sent for flowers again which was a relief. Mammy said I might well have kept my mouth shut, and maybe I did it on purpose just to get out of going for flowers.

There were other, better and more interesting things to do. Going for the meat was one, and to learn all the cuts, rib roast, silverside, porterhouse, jump steak, brisket, loin, lap, oxtail for soup, kidneys, liver and sweetbreads, and give me the bones please for the stockpot and the suet for making dripping. Fish had to be bought too, at Giblets Rea's off the Shambles, or Hazards' for fresh Ardglass herring. Or there was the procession round the wells in the town with a white enamel bucket every time the Tannaghmore supply failed. Round too to the home bakery for buns. Nobody could beat Auntie Lil for soda or wheaten bread, baked on the griddle, or Mammy for scones or flaky pastry or sponge. But neither of them could be bothered with buns so it was off in a rush for supplies into the shop, to be overwhelmed by choice and encouraged out of my indecisions by a boozy beery baker with a white apron and cap and flour-ingrained hands. 'Mamma likes a bit of colour! Mamma likes a coconut stripe!'

There were public meetings and rallies too. Old Lord Bangor, with a bushy moustache, on a platform outside the Bargain Centre in Market Street, encouraging people to subscribe to war bonds, and his wife poking him from behind with an umbrella and prodding him and telling him what to say and that he was making a mess of it and getting it all wrong and speak up and talk into the microphone, until you could hear him over the loudspeaker muttering, 'Why don't you do the bloody thing yourself.'

The Duke of Kent visited Downpatrick in a Royal Air Force uniform with so many bands and braids to show he was an air marshal; the visit was because he was Baron Downpatrick, which nobody in the town had ever heard of before. He was taken up to the cathedral to see Saint Patrick's grave and the council gave a reception for him in the big room where Daniel O'Connell had been dined by the citizens of Downpatrick. Daddy and Ned McGrady got their photographs taken and some of the councillors got very drunk, Mammy said, when the duty was off.

One of them ran down the yard, dressed up and wearing wing collar and black tie, and running so fast to keep on an even keel that he missed the way to the back gate and ran slap bang into the dung heap, which Frankie and I had to pull him out of, rubbing him down afterwards with wisps of straw and hay from the byre, his white stiff shirt front yellowed, his black suit stained and bits of straw and shit sticking to his moustache and eyebrows. James Blaney did not like it when the English papers described him as an Irish Jeeves. When the Duke of Kent was killed in an air crash not long after that, Daddy said it was a pity because he had been a civil and courteous man.

There were other deaths too, all the time, of local people on battlefields far away, and sailors lost at sea, and news at last of Billy Nolan, dead and not returning, 'killed in action', and Sam Corry, and Johnny Moore's son too, who had been in the Channel Islands, lost in France. No wonder Mr Moore was cross with stupid fools like Binney who had safe berths at home. There were two bodies washed up at Rossglass of sailors drowned at sea which had to be buried. Because Daddy was the Executive Sanitary Officer he had to see that the job was done, and they were buried in the cathedral graveyard. For some reason, or maybe for no good reason at all, only the Protestant clergyman turned up. When the coffins were ready to be carried in by the council workmen, the Catholics took cold feet and decided that they could not take part in a Protestant service. It would be a sin, or not right for them, or very unlucky, or the Canon would not like it, or something they should not do at all. Daddy tried pleading with them, but they were afraid to do it, although they would generally do anything for him – or for anyone else either, they were very decent men.

This meant there were not enough people left to carry the coffins in. Willie John Lowry and William Tuite who worked for the council and were Protestants had no problem and a couple of policemen made four. So Daddy got me to help, which I could hardly reach up to do, but he put his arm across my shoulder and took all the weight and we staggered in that way. Coming out was easier because when we got to the door the Catholic workmen, who had been waiting in the cold and dark of the evening, rushed forward and carried the coffins the rest of the way to the grave. Daddy said we had done the Christian thing to give people a decent burial and to have some prayers said for them, and he hoped somebody would do it for us some day. Mammy said she didn't think God would mind, whatever the Canon might say, and you wouldn't do it to a dog, and in any case it all came down to the one God in the end, whether you were Catholic or Protestant, Hindu or Hottentot.

On Sundays we sometimes walked up to the golf links to see the prison ship off Killyleagh, the *Al Rawdah*, anchored out in the lough with the internees on board. Daddy said it was all a lot of nonsense. They had done the same with a ship called the *Argenta* in Larne Lough years ago, but they would never learn. Most of the internees were not IRA men but silly young fellows, and the police would not know a gunman if they saw one, and they were less dangerous let out than locked up and it was all the fault of that mad old bigot Dawson Bates.

Then there was the excitement of Hugh McAteer,

the IRA chief of staff, escaping from Belfast gaol and appearing on the stage of the Broadway cinema like the Scarlet Pimpernel, until he was recaptured, they said, by a policeman who had grown up with him and saw him at communion, which didn't seem very fair. Another crowd of prisoners tunnelled out of Derry gaol and escaped in a furniture van to Donegal. And the laugh when a man on *Question Time* on Radio Éireann which we listened to faithfully every Sunday night answered 'Winston Churchill' instead of 'Hans Christian Andersen' when asked by Joe Linnane who was the world's greatest storyteller. And Mammy said, 'Oho, they won't like that.' And gathering round the Philco wireless to hear Churchill speak. And Lord Haw-Haw, night after night, intoning, 'Where is the Ark Royal?' 'Who is this Hore, Belisha?' and mocking the king with a stammer who could not speak his own English.

We said rosaries for the men who were to be hanged for shooting Constable Murphy in Belfast, and rosaries too for Constable Murphy who was only doing his job, and for his wife and little children left fatherless. And Mammy warning against secret societies and don't join anything you can't get out of, and you only leave there with a bullet in the head, either from them or somebody else, and it's wrong to kill people, and don't get tangled up with any of it, and don't listen to people with mad romantic notions, you can't eat flags or shamrocks. Joan, who was studying history, saying that every Irish rebellion had been brought down by informers and there had been more in Downpatrick than anywhere else. The United Irishmen were riddled with them, and Emmet and Russell given away, and the Fenians here and in America. And Auntie Lil maintaining that O'Connell was the great man, and Daddy saying Parnell and John Redmond, and what about Michael Collins who signed his death warrant with the Treaty?

And rosaries too for Tom Williams who was hanged in the end, and more that there would not be trouble as a result. And more too for the man from Listowel whose aunt had been Mammy's best friend, who was accused of shooting Detective Sergeant O'Brien in Dublin, and more rosaries that he would get off, and prayers from Kitty who had been at school with him and who had come up to help Mammy, and the relief and rosaries of thanksgiving when he got off through a woman in Belfast appearing in court in a black veil to swear that he had spent the night of the murder in her house. Mammy said she was glad for Nelly's sake, but it showed you the danger when decent young lads got mixed up in that sort of stuff, and somebody had done it and murder was still murder.

Mammy was getting more anxious about her sister, Aunt Nora, who had been working for years in a hotel in Bournemouth and who used to come home to us on holidays before the war. The south coast of England was within easy range of German bombers from France and there were what the English papers called 'Baedeker raids' on all the seaside resorts, called that because they were all on towns mentioned in a German travel guide. Eventually Bournemouth's Grand Hotel was bombed too and Aunt Nora came to live with us, bringing her pictures of the king and queen and the little princesses, which annoyed Auntie Lil although she would not say it to her.

Still the soldiers piled in, to the Green and Pound Lane and the racecourse and Vianstown as well as to Ballykinlar, mostly Yanks but British too, and strange regiments like the South Staffordshires and the Royal Artillery and Royal Engineers and the King's Own Scottish Borderers who, Mammy said, shot the people in Bachelor's Walk in Dublin, and airmen and WAAFs in their blue uniforms at Bishopscourt. Yanks practising dodging up and down the streets, juking into doorways, protecting each other, and tanks and lorries roaring about, the tracked vehicles cutting up the roads and making holes in the hedges as they missed corners and ploughed on through the fields and out on the other side.

Farmers prospered as tillage expanded, and more and more got tractors. There was the wonder of Double Summer Time, the clocks put back two hours in summer, extending playtime till nearly midnight, long summer evenings for hurling while the light lasted, and the walk home in a crowd in the dusk, followed by one policeman who thought we might be drilling. And the mixture of times, with us in the town on Double Summer Time, and some on just Summer Time (one hour behind Greenwich), and farmers on old time and a few still on what they called God's time, which was twenty minutes behind Greenwich. Ordinary Summer Time extended right through the winter, leaving the mornings dark and classes unable to start until half-nine because of the blackout. And on those sharp cold winter nights, in the blackout, the sky would be lit up by the magic of the Northern Lights, flickering up the dome of heaven, flashing, multi-coloured. Claire said they were called Aurora Borealis.

The Carnegie Library had been commandeered by the American Red Cross as a canteen and rest centre and the books and Mrs Cochrane had been transferred to a small room at the side of the courthouse. The Canon's Hall too was taken over by the Yanks, although after a bit the Canon got it back on Sunday nights for dancing. On other nights, if you were friendly with a Yank you could get smuggled in when the troops were being entertained: film stars, singers, comedians and Joe Louis in an exhibition bout with Billy Conn, and hundreds of soldiers shouting and roaring and cheering.

The British had shows too, given by ENSA, the organisation of artists engaged to entertain the troops, in the town hall. The performers often came to eat in the hotel during the day when they were rehearsing, and spent most of the time in the bar drinking. They would get you into a show through the Minor Hall and up the back stairs; I saw a play called *Private Lives* by Noël Coward, which was much different to *The Auction at Killybuck* or *Thompson in Tir na nOg*.

The old gun in the Mall was taken away for scrap, to be melted down and fired back at the Germans, I supposed. So too were all the iron gates and railings, beautiful wrought iron, cut down and carted off, Daddy said, to finish up in a heap rusting on the docks in Belfast.

In school, in addition to people from schools in Belfast evacuated after the blitz, some of whom stayed until the end of the war, there were the Gibraltarians. These people arrived in the middle of the war when all the civilians were removed from the Rock of Gibraltar, where Bill Boal in Killough had got his clock set into a piece of the stone, and a photograph of the Rock with a big notch on top to show you where the stone came out of.

The Gibraltarians arrived in the cold and wet and were put into Nissen huts hastily erected in fields along the road at Cargagh Cut and Clough, which the Yanks called Clow and the English Cluff. You would see the Gibraltarians in little groups around the town, more swarthy than most, keeping to themselves, huddled for warmth on the lee side of corners out of the wind. The women made some money selling crocheted and knitted garments to the shops, but most of the time they had nothing to do. A Spanish-speaking priest called Father Murphy used to say mass for them; he had an ulcer and Mammy used to get him olive oil without coupons.

To our surprise, some of the Gibraltarian boys who came to school had Irish and English names – they were the children of Spanish mothers and British servicemen over the ages. So we had Juan Manuel McEwan, Jesu Maria Powell, Miguel McIntyre and Jiminez Kelly. They spoke Spanish to each other and taught us to count in Spanish: *uno, dos, tres, cuatro, cinco* . . . and some Spanish words like *cojones* and *puta* which turned out to be not at all polite.

Cassidys' too was getting busier as the troops left their boots in to be repaired, and now there were long lines of machines where before there had been a single cobbler, machines driven by whirring belts along the wall, more like a factory, not like Mr Waterman who stuck to his last. There was a side of leather hung out every morning on a nail beside the door bearing the chalk-written message 'Shoes soled and heeled while

U wait'. One day an angry customer complained that his shoes were still not ready after two or three days and pointed accusingly to the notice. Old Mr Cassidy did not pay much heed. 'Well, you're waiting, aren't you?' was all he would say.

And then all of a sudden the troops disappeared, having first piled all the bikes they had bought in a heap at the racecourse and run tanks over them and we thought it was a great waste when you could not even get spare parts for bicycles. The next we heard of them, they were invading North Africa.

But soon there were more and more soldiers with every place filled up with troops, preparing, it was clear, for the the invasion of Europe. Charlie Leathem won a medal for bravery for having made more flights as a rear gunner on a pathfinder bomber over Germany than anybody else, and there was a big do in the town hall. Bishopscourt was expanded again and General Eisenhower landed there. The new, longer runway extended across a bog; as it as being built an old farmer leaned over the ditch to remark that it was so deep it could never be bottomed. He was told arrogantly, 'We'll bottom it with dollars.' Cassidys' machines continued to whirr away as the boots came flooding in to be mended, and there was not an unploughed field in the country, not a patch of waste ground that did not have a Nissen hut on it, or a tank or a mobile gun under a camouflage netting. There were soldiers everywhere on manoeuvres, a dozen of them drowned trying to get a flat-bottomed boat across the Bar of Dundrum, a plane crashed at Coney Island, and the pilot drowned as the water rose. The bystanders could only stand and watch, unable to get him out. And ships were wrecked all along the coast, caught in the spring gales as they lined up for convoy duty.

EIGHTEEN

EVEN IN WARTIME, SCHOOL WAS HUMDRUM enough most of the time – not much more than eighty or ninety boys in six classes, the classes getting smaller as the pupils in them grew larger. Boys fell out to go into the family business, or to work on the farm or to get work in one of the industries or the building sites or to learn a trade or because their families were hard pressed or they were not going to make it academically or they were fed up with the discipline and being treated like children, or whatever.

Discipline was strict, but not oppressive. All the teachers had canes, but most did not use them regularly. The Brothers had leather straps about fifteen inches long hanging down inside their soutanes; some of them drew the straps like a gunslinger in a western film and waded into pupils when they were in bad form or had lost their patience with indolence or crass stupidity. The boys who had come from Belfast said it was a doddle after the Christian Brothers who used the

strap all the time and sewed coins up between the
layers of leather to make it more painful. Most of the
teachers used their hands impulsively, with a cuff on
the ear or a knuckled blow on the skull or slaps around
the legs of the younger boys who wore short trousers.
Or the odd kick. The most wounding weapon was sar-
casm, criticism in front of the class, mockery of weak-
ness or inadequacy, comparison with boys who had
done well, or others who had done badly and disgraced
themselves and their families. Nobody thought this
strange. You were there to work and they were there
to make you and that was all there was to it.

The outstanding character for all this time was the
headmaster, who also taught English, Brother Edmund
Murphy, from Kishkeam in the County Cork. He was
a flamboyant figure both inside and outside the school,
with a wide range of interests and bizarre notions on almost every subject. His nickname was Aubrey, a corruption of 'Abair é', the Irish for 'Say it!' He used this
phrase continually, going round the school in the attempt to encourage boys to speak Irish, or at least to
use Gaelic words and phrases. He wore a long cloak
over his soutane as he walked to and from school, with
an umbrella in one hand and swinging a Gladstone bag
in the other, wearing a flat, broad-brimmed hat which
made him look like the silhouette of the man on the
advertisement for Sandeman's port. He was interested
in greyhounds, which he had bred and trained on a
previous posting, and in herbal remedies for which he
exchanged recipes and specifics with old bearded Mr
Green who ran the little gospel hall at the back of
Bridge Street. Brother Murphy was a keen walker,
covering miles on a Sunday afternoon, and a good

handballer who could be seen cycling to alleys round the country looking for somebody good enough to give him a game.

Aubrey's great interest, and his greatest joy, was in linguistics, especially the Irish language. He was convinced that the revival of Irish as the spoken language of everyday use, which he keenly desired, was being impeded by the difficulty of the language, by the conflict between dialects and their supporters, by the difficulty presented to the learner by grammatical forms and inflexions, by declensions and irregular forms, by the complicated spelling and an antique script that could not be used on a typewriter and by highly eccentric idioms and usages. Typically he cut through all this and invented a new form of Irish called Eeris which had none of these things – no irregularities, no inflexions, no idioms – in which all was standardised and words were spelled as they sounded and written in Roman script with a *h* inserted for an aspiration and a double vowel for an accent. He ran a one-man campaign against all the vested interests – against the teaching profession, against the Gaelic League and the language purists, against the Irish government which would not take action, against the native speakers whom he saw as pedantic backwoodsmen, against the language enthusiasts who wished to preserve not only the language (in a petrified and unchangeable form) but the dialects in which they abused each other and fought battles about purity and authenticity. He conducted his campaign by means of public meetings, to which a few cowed members of staff came, and some boys sent out by their mothers, and a few disciples whom he had recruited, and a handful of curious bystanders who had nothing else to do for an hour or could think of no better way to pass the time. He also ran classes in Eeris, usually on a Sunday morning when the school was deserted, which you only went to because you might be excused an essay for Monday, or might get away with four pages instead of six.

Mostly, however, Edmund worked through letters to the newspapers, both daily and weekly, which he submitted for publication in the names of one or other of his disciples. So that a man baling hay on a farm in Lecale, or working on a building site, or minding his shop, might be surprised to open the *Irish News* some morning and find himself the author of a long and learned discussion on comparative philology. There was an unexpected bonus in this for me too, a sort of finder's fee. Among the papers to which he regularly sent letters were the *Kerryman* and the *Waterford Star,* both of which were posted every week to Daddy and Mammy. When Aubrey had written a letter to one or other and was awaiting publication, he would ask me to look out for it and bring the paper in to him. This meant that on those days, you could come back, bearing the paper, to school after lunch a few minutes late but without fear of the strap, the usual retribution for lateness.

In his attitude to the Irish language, as in many other ways, Edmund was a man ahead of his time. Years later, Irish spelling was indeed standardised along the lines he had suggested, if not quite so radically, by the very people who had vilified him most. The script was changed too, but nobody gives him any credit and Eeris is a memory only for the very few.

Edmund made us try out his linguistic theories, which made classes an adventure in verbal and grammatical exploration. For some reason, the Our Father was the test-bed for most of these theories: I must have written out the Lord's Prayer more times and in more forms than any medieval monk in his scriptorium – in Ogham, in four dialects of Irish, in Manx and Scots Gaelic, in Basic English, Esperanto, Volapuk and Occidental, and in any other language fad that came along.

Edmund was an interesting and eccentric teacher. He had come to the conclusion that all the information needed to answer the Junior and Senior Certificate examination questions could be summarised on four stencilled sheets, and he supplied these with orders to learn them off by heart, after which he proceeded to educate by means of moral disquisitions and Socratic questioning based on the texts under study. Who did Lord George Gordon, in *Barnaby Rudge*, the instigator of the Gordon Riots, remind us of, and what was the difference between anti-Catholic riots in Bath in 1767 and riots in Belfast in the 1930s? What had Henry v to say about the responsibility of the general for the deaths of soldiers in war that Churchill and other leaders might well think about, and what did that say about what was going on in the world? Edmund had a few hobbyhorses: drink, smoking, golf, international finance, the popular press and sex, all of which were to be avoided at all costs. What for instance did we think of the propriety of Maggie Tulliver in *The Mill on the Floss* going out in a boat alone with a boy?

This was all a bit above the head of a boy younger by a year or two than most of his classmates, who had been saved from death by meningitis at the age of seven by rosaries and novenas and water from holy wells, and relics, and hands laid on by a newly ordained priest who had gone off to the missions and kept claiming his dealing trick by letters expressing the belief that I had been spared to follow him. All of which produced a sort of pressure that I would at least try to follow that route, the end of which was celibacy and which tended to restrict relationships with girls to chaste correctness, even if it had been in my mind to do other. I did not see what the difficulty was with Maggie Tulliver. After all, you could quite safely go out with a girl in a rowboat in Killough provided she could row – which most of them could not, so maybe that was the problem.

In the aisling poems in Irish, which Edmund also taught, the reward the poet promised the downtrodden and dispossessed Irish was that the oppressors would be expelled by French or Spanish help. Victory would be symbolised by Charles Stuart, the Young Pretender, lying down with Ireland in one of her female personifications – Gráinne Mhaol, Cathleen Ni Houlihan, or Deirdre or Banba. This seemed to me at the time to be a poor and undramatic outcome for such a lot of effort.

Sex was anything but rampant. Missioners continued to thunder about the immorality of films, but even the lurid posters of the female stars stuck on the walls of the cinema disappeared because of the paper shortage as the war went on. These were replaced by other advertisements on walls and in the papers warning of the dangers of venereal disease, whatever that was, and describing in explicit detail how to recognise the symptoms – 'a mucuo-purous emission from the sexual membrane'. The other posters, signed Fougasse, saying 'Careless talk costs lives' with a cartoon of a little man's nose sticking over a wall, were funnier, and much easier to get the point of.

Posters and films and missioners aside, at that time sex was a succession of furtive, ill-understood allusions, or pretending to laugh at the odd dirty joke, and embarrassment at failure to understand it, or wonder at night emissions or day-time erections, shame-making during PT. Older boys sniggered when boasting about hiding in the bushes at the Steamboat Quay to watch the French girl who was staying with the Newmans as she undressed to go swimming, and you suspected that not only had they not done so, but they had not done much else in the sex business either.

I remember walking along the Circular Road to devotions one warm Friday evening in the summer when an older boy explained the mechanics of sex to me in terms of the man sticking his pen into the woman's inkpot. This was a lot less romantic than Charles Stuart lying down with Gráinne Mhaol, which I had thought to be sufficient for procreation – a sort of impregnation by proximity – and not very much more practical. If only somebody had told me that it was the same, in principle, as bringing Millie and Angeline to Bohills' bull, life would have been much simpler.

In fairness, Edmund did make his own effort at sex education. When he thought a boy was ready for it he brought him into his office and gave him a private talk on the facts of life. He read these from a text on a sheaf of typed sheets which was known by the boys as 'the yellow pages' or 'the eight pages'. Boys were seen to go in uncomfortably to the office, and later to come out embarrassedly, sidling away from any challenge, although some boasted that the dirty details were not news to them. My turn came when I had progressed into the senior class, though I was still not far into puberty. It was an ordeal. Sitting on a high bentwood chair, with legs so short that my feet dangled a few inches from the floor, was bad enough. Trying to avoid eye contact with Edmund, and assenting to every proposition that he put in order to bring the interview to an end made it worse. We spent a long time on the pollination of plants, on stamens and pistils, on the vital function of the honey bee, the danger of infection and disease, the awful punishment God visited on transgressors, and the need to avoid girls at all costs, all of which left me with the impression that sex was a complicated matter, more trouble than it was worth, and liable to get you stung.

Edmund's other penchant, besides the Irish language, was for great engineering works carried out manually by the boys. Most of the maintenance work in the school was done by the Brothers, and they kept the grounds in order too. You would see Brothers in shirtsleeves with spades and shovels and slashers and scythes and billhooks cleaning the grounds in the afternoon and at weekends. Sometimes Edmund would burst into a class and conscript two or three boys to dig channels down the bank to relieve flooding, or to clear blocked drains, or to chase invading sheep and cattle off the grounds and to repair the holes in the fences that had let them in.

His greatest enterprise was to level the playing field, which had a steep hill in one corner. This he tackled

with pick and shovel, helped by groups of boys
pressed into service in free periods, at lunch time, or
after school, like ants in formation, shovelling, filling
buckets, carrying them aside, and dumping them in
the wheelbarrow. Edmund would be there, soutane
tails tucked into his belt, swinging a pick as others
shovelled the loosened shale into wheelbarrows to be
wheeled heavily and unsteadily away and dumped in
holes in the hedge or in hollows in the boundary ditch.
Sometimes at weekends he recruited a friendly builder
to place charges of dynamite here and there to loosen
the shale where the rock ran near the surface, leaving it
in rippled layers to be hoked out and removed by the
army of ants in the following week. Progress was
painfully slow, like building the Pyramids or the Great
Wall of China: nothing to show for a day's work, or
for a week's, little enough even after a month, but yet
he persevered on a project extending over a couple of
years until in the end there was a relatively level playing pitch produced by human hands and sweat.

There were fund-raising events too, sports days
with visiting football and hurling teams and boxing
contests fought out in a ring hastily erected on the
grass, and donkey rides and athletic exhibitions and
orations and lectures in the open air and Irish dancing
and elocution contests and side shows and roulette and
hoop-la and every means of taking money off people
to finance the running of the school where there were
very few state scholarships. The Brothers worked for
nothing and the teachers for not much more, and the
fees were very low.

Edmund interested some horsy people in running a
gymkhana at the school to make money. Because of

the war and the shortage of petrol and an outbreak of foot-and-mouth disease in the South, it was not possible to bring horses to the Dublin Horse Show or to Balmoral and the school gymkhana became a great social event. True, it did not have the tent-pegging and the fiercely contested polo matches we were familiar with from films set on the North-West Frontier and in the Indian Raj, but for us it was strange and exotic, and it brought some odd people round the school.

Again schoolboy labour was pressed into service to help men with corduroy jodhpurs and hacking jackets who came in to supervise the building of fences and stone walls and banks for the jumping. Tommy Dougherty was in his element as a man who really knew the business, although the real experts seemed to ignore him. There was also a track to be roped off and flags to be put up and tents and marquees to be borrowed from the army. Hundreds of people turned up with high-class horses, Lady Mari Bury from Mount Stewart, and Mrs Garland from Newry, and the Willises and Bambers and other hunting and show-jumping people and Miss Barbara Falloon from Warrenpoint on her champion pony Golden Lass. There were fabulous horses there, like Quicksilver and Ballyblack and Rainbow Chaser who established the world record for the Champion Stone Wall in Downpatrick and was photographed doing so in all the papers, soaring like a bird against the clouds, miles to spare over the top of the wall.

I was recruited to help the judges record the marks: four faults for a front foot fault, three for knocking off a pole or dislodging a stone with a trailing leg, four for a refusal, disqualified by the sound of a handbell rung vigorously by me when the number of faults climbed into the high teens. This was a really cushy job as the judges were well supplied with drinks and tea and cakes, and after a couple of years I got quite good at it. The prizes were substantial, huge by our standards, especially for just jumping fences which horses were inclined to do by nature anyhow: £7 for the jumping and £10 for the Champion Stone Wall. But the third year Edmund decided that this was far too much to pay for jumping over a wall and he took half the money out of the prize envelopes without changing the amounts on the outside or telling the judges or anybody else. The winners all went away thinking they had won twice as much as they carried with them and there was a terrible row when they found out that they had been short-changed. Ray said that was the end of Edmund and it wouldn't be long until he was shifted.

The teaching we received was fairly basic, poetry learned off by heart, other texts too, with much reliance on the written word. There were written exercises in most subjects every night, despite air raids and ARP duties, as well as learning-off, and long essays to be written at weekends. Maths and science were a bit difficult because of Edmund's inability to get on with maths teachers; they came and went with great regularity. Latin and Irish were taught as grammatical exercises and as equally dead languages with no feeling for literature, although the use of Latin at mass and in the missal did give it a romance and a currency it might not otherwise have had. Later I regretted that Caesar's Gallic wars had been presented to us as cowboys-and-Indians with Caesar and the Romans as the goodies. It was years later that I came to realise that the Gauls were Celts. like Celtair, that the Dun of Down resonated in their place names, and that I had more in common with them, and indeed with the Red Indians and other dispossessed people, than with Caesar. Nobody ever thought either that a visit to the Mount might have helped us to visualise the fortifications at Alesia, although I did use it as my private frame of reference. There was no sense either that Horace was poetry that just might be fun, or that Ovid's *Metamorphoses* was about magic. Irish poetry too was dead on the page until I heard Martin Gleeson from south Tipperary, spoke-shaving a shaft for a cart under the great chestnut tree in the council yard, recite me an English version of 'Cáit á Gará na' Bhile':

> Have you been in Garanavilla?
> Have you seen in Garanavilla
> Beauty's train trip o'er the plain
> With lovely Kate of Garanavilla?

And Eamonn Mac Giolla Iasachta became honest Ned Lysaght, a poet and a lively man who loved a lady. A book called *Peig* anchored Irish firmly with so many words and phrases that were on Mammy's lips all the time, and Daddy told me that his mother in Waterford was a native speaker, but she never spoke Irish to the children, keeping this as a secret language for the grown-ups.

History was the history of England, of kings and dynasties and wars and rebellions and social and economic and constitutional change there and in the Empire. European history was taught from an English viewpoint because that was what the text books did.

Irish history was avoided as something that would get you into trouble at exams if the examiners for the Ministry did not like what you were saying and marked you down as a result.

Instead, Irish history became something to be absorbed almost from folklore, from the yearly issue of the *Capuchin Annual*, banned one year because the government did not like it, but smuggled in none the less, and the *Wolfe Tone Annual* received every year from Kerry despite health warnings from Mammy about the damaging effects of romantic republicanism. Irish history was also mugged up from texts by Mrs Helena Concannon in order to win cash prizes at the Newcastle Feis (pronounced Faish in County Down). There were also competitions, and prizes for Irish speaking, for collecting place names, for storytelling and for essays on local history. The Newcastle Feis was held in the park where the children on the Canon's Excursion had their lunch and tea and it was marked by boring and tedious orations, always beginning with a few words in Irish by some pompous worthy, who threw in a lot of incomprehensible phrases which sounded mysterious like 'racy of the soil' and 'on his keeping', the latter apparently meaning 'on the run'. The only things that brightened up the day and created any excitement were seven-a-side matches Gaelic football and hurling.

There was no library in the school. At least, there was a room marked 'Library' which was also the tea room, with shelves along one wall but no books to borrow or even to browse through. Salvation was found in the Carnegie Library, whose ticket gave unlimited access to Edgar Wallace, Jack London,

Stephen Leacock, Freeman Wills Crofts, Arnold Bennett, J.B. Priestley, Owen Francis Dudley and a host of others. There were books at home too: Daddy's set of Dickens, and Walter Scott and a bound volume of Shakespeare, which Auntie Lil knew off by heart, and books that the others had had at school and discarded.

I once told Edmund about a writer who was living at the Inch called Magdalen King-Hall. She was married to one of the Maxwells of Finnebrogue and her brother was a Member of Parliament who broadcast frequently on the radio. Edmund asked me if I had read her books and I said yes and offered to get him one from the library. I had read one called *The Lady Sarah* which was tame enough. The one I got out was called *The Wicked Lady*. Unfortunately I had not the time to read the book before giving it to him. When he handed it back he gave me an odd look and asked me if I had read it. I said I had and that it was very enjoyable. His look became even odder. When I did read the book I discovered it was full of female adventuresses with very loose morals and men who were no better.

Edmund brought all sorts of strange people to the school – including strolling players and unemployed actors who played out bits of whatever Shakespeare play we were studying and brought it to life. He brought faith-healers and storytellers and sound men and eccentrics. There was an old soldier from Liverpool who had been shot so many times at the Somme and had caught so many pieces of shrapnel that he rattled when he walked. He had survived, he believed, through the intervention of Our Lady and he had become a *brancardier* at Lourdes, carrying the sick to the baths, and had dedicated his life to spreading the message of Lourdes. Once there was a priest who was also a hypnotist. He boasted that he could get any boy through an exam, provided he had ever read the book, by bringing the information up to the surface of his mind in a hypnotic trance, back from the recesses of his memory. He also said that he could hypnotise any rational person, anybody except an infant or a lunatic. Later Edmund came into the class boasting that the priest had been able to hypnotise all the other Brothers except himself. He thought this was a tribute to his strength of will, and wondered why we thought that was funny.

Then there was the radio, to be listened to for the news and for Lord Haw-Haw. To make sure that people knew it was them, the BBC announcers began to give their names before reading the news, and on a Sunday night before the nine o'clock news they played the national anthems of the allied countries, which became a bit tedious as country after country fell to the Germans or the Japanese. There were the weekly serials, *Dick Barton, Special Agent, The Man in Black, In Town Tonight* ('Once more we stop the roar of London traffic to bring you the interesting people who are *in town tonight!*'). And *Question Time* on Radio Éireann and Michael O'Hehir describing football and hurling matches and helping you to visualise the pitch by referring to square three and square four and so on.

The cinema too was a big educator, crowded most of the time, with long queues round Breens' corner for the two shows a night and matinées on Monday and Saturday. I was allowed go to the early house on a

Friday, and on a Monday for an extra-special film. I was able to skip the queues by going down through the back gate and slipping in through a side door and up to the balcony where Mr Breen kept a few seats for his friends. This gave unlimited access to westerns, to romantic pictures about the British Empire like *Gunga Din*, to Chicago gangland with James Cagney and Edward G. Robinson, and to Boys' Town, with Spencer Tracy and Mickey Rooney; it allowed me to meet Judy Garland in St Louis, and Greer Garson as Mrs Miniver organising the evacuation from Dunkirk on her own. There was Gary Cooper as Sergeant York, shooting Germans like ducks in Tennessee, putting a drop of spittle on his front sight with his thumb in defiance of army training, but outshooting them all and quoting scripture at the same time. And Scarlett O'Hara in the blazing ruins of Atlanta and Robert Taylor playing rugby with the best of them in *A Yank at Oxford*.

Because of the shortage of equipment in the science room, there were always bits and pieces to be improvised or borrowed from the town's Protestant school, the Green High, and I used to be sent there for supplies at lunch time, up Wallace's Lane and through the great granite arch of the gateway, wheeling a bicycle up to the front door. The headmaster's office was on the right just inside the door, and the science master was acting head because the headmaster was away at the war. The master was a gentle courteous man called by everybody Tommy Stevenson, and I got to like going up to him for messages. One day, however, as I stood outside the office door and knocked, with an empty Winchester bottle in my gloved hands in which to borrow distilled water, the door swung open suddenly and a man with a military moustache in a mortarboard and swishing gown stood in front of me. This was the headmaster, back from his bomb disposal squad to take up teaching again. He was a nice man too, but I was so startled that the bottle shot from my hand and shattered itself against a radiator just inside the door. Immediately I was down on my knees, mumbling apologies and picking up pieces of broken glass. He got down too to help me pick it up, assuring me that it was an accident and that he would speak to Brother Edmund and I would not be punished. He did not know that it was not the fear of punishment that distressed me, but the fact that I had let the side down: that a Catholic boy had made an idiot of himself in the Protestant school.

NINETEEN

THE BUSINESS IN THE HOTEL WAS NOW WELL established. Despite the difficulties of rationing and controls and short supplies and quotas and coupons and permits and licences, my mother had built up a good trade in both the bar and the restaurant, and the hotel rooms were permanently full. Ray was now working in the civil service, and at night and at weekends in the bar and bottling and other jobs about the hotel. Joan was at university and working part-time in the Inland Revenue. Claire was a probationer nurse in Belfast having got over the shock of her first week of duty during the Blitz in one of the worst-hit parts of the city, and the loss of her clothes and possessions when the nurses' home was bombed. Carmel and Helen were at a boarding school in Lisburn and I used to get a ride over in Charlie Thompson's taxi when he was leaving them back after the holidays. Once one of the nuns at the school asked me coyly whether I had a vocation, and when I stammered in confusion that maybe I might,

she led me down a corridor and showed me into the
toilets. There would also be tea in the parlour which
had on the walls a couple of beautiful paintings by Sir
John Lavery of which the nuns were very proud. An
old nun in the convent was his aunt, or some relation
anyhow. The pictures were not religious, and much
better than the sunburst Sacred Hearts or the stark
Crucifixions or the soppy Madonnas in the framed
prints in the convent in Downpatrick. The nuns wore
a strange, closed starched headgear called a coif which
almost concealed their faces and they looked as if they
were peeping out at you through a crack in the curtains. It was very different from the gear the nuns
wore in Downpatrick which was much more open
and showed the face but not the hair, a sort of wimple
like the dress of the women in the illustrated edition of
The Canterbury Tales.

Mammy had made a lot of improvements to the
hotel. For one thing, the drab dirty dark grey outside,
with damp showing through in patches and cracked
and peeling plaster with the woodwork showing bare
and bleached through chipped paint, was transformed.
She had it all painted in a bright sharp lemon shade
which made the place look bigger and lit up the whole
street. The windows were painted in deep maroon and
the bottom of the wall in brown so as not to show the
dust, and the front door and the great yard gate
were grained to simulate mahogany and brightly
varnished. Across the front of the recessed bay, under
the drawing-room windows, MAGEE'S HOTEL was
painted out and Mr Chambers painted DENVIR'S
HOTEL in Roman capitals with serifs and shading.
Old Miss Denvir was so pleased she brought Mammy

in a chicken and a pound of country butter, and she kept sending us country butter every week for years. Mr Chambers also painted HOTEL on the big chimney, and vertically down the wall so that it could be seen from the town hall and by people coming up the street. Over the door, in small precise letters, he painted the legend: 'Margaret Hayes, licensed to sell beer, wine, spirits and tobacco for consumption on or off the premises.' The brass door handle, the knocker and the letterbox were polished each morning with Brasso, which made them shine but also left a trace of white chalk in the grooves and round the edges where it could not be polished off, or where the rubbing had removed some of the varnish.

Inside, the colour scheme was changed from the drab two-tone green distemper on the stairs and the dark, smoke-stained and peeling varnish on the wooden wainscoting. There were bright colours everywhere, rooms papered and painted, ceilings lined in anaglypta and floors stained and new linoleum laid, and all at a time when things were scarce, timber had to be begged, paint was nearly unobtainable and tradesmen were hard to get because there was so much work at the camps. We all helped. I turned my hand to much of the routine maintenance, mainly through watching tradesmen and copying what they did, fixing electricity, replacing bulbs, doing minor joinery repairs, putting in the screw or the nail that would prevent further damage, replacing broken cords in sash windows, doing rough papering and painting where it didn't matter too much, like our own side of the house over the gateway. Frankie and his father whitewashed the yard and the outhouses every year with lime slaked for days in a barrel covered with a bag until it stopped bubbling and spitting, and they put a black border round the base with tar from the gasworks.

Mammy was always pleased when you mended something or did a bit of joinery because it reminded her of her father in Kerry who had been a carpenter. After inspecting a job well done, she would call me the Gobán Saor after a legendary Celtic artificer and fixer. She was great at letting you get on with the job without interference provided you got down to it. She would wait for the finished product and operated according to the maxim that you should not keep a dog and bark yourself. I worked a lot in the kitchen with her too because I was ambidextrous and could put two bits of garnish on a plate at the same time and did not get in her way when she was carving.

She was delighted when the new crockery arrived. Like the name over the door, it changed the pattern and stamped her image on the place. There was a black crest, which she had chosen, on a white background on each piece, plates, cups, saucers and vegetable dishes. The ware came packed in tea-chests, each piece wrapped separately and packed in shavings, from Dunn Bennett & Co., Burslem, Staffordshire. I had read, first of all, *Anna of the Five Towns* and then most of Arnold Bennett's books and I knew about the Potteries, but this brought it all nearer. There was new cutlery too, from Sheffield, which had to be polished and cleaned by hand, not insulted by being put into James Blaney's knife-cleaning machine which was put down into the store. There was a new Esse cooker too, installed like a military manoeuvre so as to interfere as little as possible with the serving of meals, but which transformed the kitchen and warmed the whole house during the night. It also created the problem of getting supplies of Welsh anthracite which was very scarce, and a new job for Ray, night and morning to stoke the fire and rake out the red-hot ashes. The kitchen continued to be dominated by the great dresser stretching along one wall from door to door, which displayed Mammy's willow-pattern plates and carving dishes.

Ray took me to see a soccer match in Belfast at which the British Army played Ireland. There was a frightening crush up some iron stairs over a railway line, and worse coming down on the other side. Ray protected me by putting his arms on either side of me and pressing his hands against the wall, but I didn't want ever to go there again. The army goalkeeper was a big man called Swift with huge hands who could throw the ball from one end of the pitch to the other. The great man on the Irish side was called Bertie Fulton who was a friend of Auntie Lil's when she worked in Larne.

In addition there were the plays in the town hall and in the Canon's Hall and amateur operettas and concerts. The school put on plays, including a version of Molière called *The Mock Doctor*. I seemed always to get a female part and in the Molière play that came in very handy since I had to slap the face of a male character. He was a bigger boy who had tripped me from behind and cut my chin when the school was up in Irish Street, so I slapped his face with great delight and some force. In *Thompson in Tir na nOg*, however, I was able to play the lead role, having had the advantage of having seen the part played by Willie McAllister in the Hib Hall in Killough so many times that I could remember the words.

Mainly, however, it was reading and access to books that kept me going. Books from school, books from the Carnegie Library, books borrowed from lending libraries in the shops, books dropped by Mammy when she fell asleep reading them before her afternoon nap. She did not always want me to read them, but never stopped me once I had started one. Mostly she was into Annie M.P. Smithson and Marie Corelli. The girls too had books, *Anne of Green Gables, Little Women* and *The Little House on the Prairie*. There was Auntie Lil, ceaselessly doing crossword puzzles and word games and competitions, and waiting until I came in from school to check a clue. There were weekly magazines and comics. There were newspapers of every kind and opinion, brought in by customers and left behind.

There was also conversation, in the bar, in the kitchen, at the meal table which we all sat round in our appointed places. Each had his or her own two ounces of rationed butter to be scraped off the paper, or a pot of jam rinsed out with a spoonful of warm water to get the last raspberry seed out. Everybody was free to raise any subject or to take part in the conversation or to bring their own story or news. The only problem was ridicule, to be laughed at, or cut to the bone with a harsh word or sharp wit. There were prayers at night too, immediately after the tea, chairs turned around, everybody on their knees, and Mammy adding special requests to the stock list as the state of the world or the war, or the family or our health or some exam or other caused her concern.

It cannot be that the summers were endlessly and unfailingly fine and sunny, but that is the way they seemed. There were a few better-than-average summers when tillage had been pushed to the extreme limits and you could always find a farmer glad of help with the hay or the harvest or the flax-pulling and retting. Double Summer Time made the evenings endless, and the winters too were exceptional – cold, but seasonal in a romantic sort of way, the marshes frozen for skating, and the Quoile too, right across so that it could be walked over at Jane's Shore by a couple of hardy souls who could never have heard of the seven-year curse, or Stanley Smyth, or poor Florrie Mearns, drowned on the ice in Cochrane's Bog.

There was, too, the delight of football, both impromptu and organised, and the sheer delight of hurling, of being able to pull on a ball dropping from the sky, or to double on a rolling ball on the ground, to lift, to block, to feint, to sidestep, the mastery of the carried ball and the skill to raise a sideline cut thirty, forty, fifty yards through the air. There was the excitement of tournaments played in or watched. Travelling by bicycle to country pitches, no markings, no dressing rooms but the thorn hedge, to carnival and *aeraíocht*s (outdoor sports meetings with dancing and music) that punctuated the summer, Sunday after Sunday. The rush and clamour of crowds in unfenced fields, the barely repressed violence as partisans roared their teams on, the simmering threat of physical attack on referees and umpires, and the frequent bouts of fisticuffs on and off the pitch which threatened to degenerate into fracas. Daddy did not like this at all. He would say to somebody, 'They never change', and go off home. If you kept out of range you could watch it all and learn to identify those most likely to raise a row, the ladies with swinging handbags who would accost a referee or have a go at a linesman, the sideline lawyers with rule books ready to win in the committee room on a technicality a match that had been lost on the field. It was all raw and vital and immediate.

There were tug-of-war matches, refereed by a big man who had been a high-jump champion and who was reputed to have cleared the wall out of an English gaol with de Valera and Michael Collins. But that did not stop him being abused by the overweight members of a team disqualified for persistently lying on the rope.

As the Americans arrived in ever greater numbers, the tide of the war had changed. The Allies had started to win. North Africa had been captured and half of Italy, including Rome. Bombing raids on Germany were reported more and more often, raids on Britain less and less. There was rumoured to be a secret weapon. Daddy said it was all now just a matter of time. There would be a second front in Europe when the Russians had lost enough men for them not to be a threat after the war. The Americans would carry the invasion by weight of armament and force of numbers. Then, one morning, all the Americans, all the planes, all the ships, were gone – off to France to end the war. And then there was a plot against Hitler which Daddy said was the beginning of the end. Hitler was a madman and the military would ditch him and look for the best deal they could get.

My schooling too had reached a turning point. My days at the Red High were drawing to a close. True to form, Edmund produced the leather on my last day and slapped me for some minor infraction which I do not now remember. I do remember the indignity of the parting shot. There were eight of us left in the class who took the Senior examination. Having been together, and seen others fall out, we were now parting and going different ways. My last memory is of a sports day on the last day at the end of the school year, winning three races and getting a couple of awful books as prizes, *My New Curate* by Canon Sheehan, which was stodgy enough, and *The Way of Perfection for the Laity*, which was unreadable, uninviting, unattainable. Mr Johnston was very cross about my running in the 220 yards race. He claimed to have been a better-than-average sprinter in his youth, and to have watched some of the best, including Willie Kelly, and he wanted to know why I had looked round over my shoulder when near the tape. I said I had just wanted to see how far behind the others were. He replied that was no way to run a race, or to do anything else. Keep your eyes on the finish, keep the goal in your mind and go for it, without distraction. Single-minded, that's what you had to be.

The warmest memory is of walking out the road with three classmates to leave a fourth boy part of the way home to Rosconnor. We intended first to go only as far as the war memorial, then we extended our escort in stages to the Quoile Bridge and Finnebrogue gates and Skillen's Pike and up the hill, finally to where the road crosses the railway line at King's Bridge. There we stood talking in the long twilight, leaning against the parapet, watching the rails on their sleepers stretch back towards the loop line, and turning to see them stretch out to somewhere, parallel we knew, and never meeting, but the perspective defeated geometry and the lines did meet away out there and pointed towards some unknown and indeterminate future.

We walked back past the bewitched pillars, gateless behind the wall at Finnebrogue, round the road in the gathering dusk, the northern sky still bright almost till midnight and never quite dark. As we passed the sign saying one mile to the Inch, I sensed that the time had come to fold up the large-scale local map with its intimate and revealing detail, to put it away in the drawer of memory, and to take down the map of the world. This was more likely to resemble Ptolemy's rather than Mercator's projection, full of unexplored spaces, with fudged outlines and uncertain landmarks and a few imprecisely located destinations, and around the edges all sorts of strange, grotesque and menacing creatures. Then back into the town and home.

ALSO BY

MAURICE HAYES

SWEET KILLOUGH, LET GO YOUR ANCHOR

'Memories of life in the thirties in a Co. Down village, and quite unlike many such recollections, because this one is not just vivid, it is also a book of humour, imagination and re-creation. It is evocative in a way that few books are ... will make you open your eyes again to a world that has disappeared, but has not been forgotten.'

SEAN McCANN, *EVENING PRESS*

'a personal and passionate history of a small place by a big-hearted and sharp-minded man who combines the mental objectivity of a good historian with the intensity of a lyric poet ... Maurice Hayes has produced a minor masterpiece ...'

BRENDAN KENNELLY, *IRISH INDEPENDENT*

'If there is a more magical album of childhood memories, real or fantasy, I would like to know what it is.'

CHRIS PATTEN, *FINANCIAL TIMES*

'It should surely go into the annals of local history, to be read and cherished by future generations.'

TIM CRAMER, *CORK EXAMINER*

'In these pages, Killough has the documentary realism of Joyce's Dublin and the emotional security of Goldsmith's Auburn ... there is a beautiful convergence of the quotidian and the uncanny.'

SEAMUS HEANEY

pb; 210 x 135 mm; 232 pp; illus.; £7.99
0-85640-528-0

MINORITY VERDICT
EXPERIENCES OF A CATHOLIC PUBLIC SERVANT

'Many good books have come out of the troubles in the North, but this is one of the most elegant, well-informed and trenchant. Maurice Hayes's position as a senior civil servant at Stormont *malgré lui* gave him a unique insight into the crumbling edifice left by 50 years of unionist rule. His inside account of the convoluted business of trying to create new political structures on the basis of old prejudices, and the oddity of many of the bods who came over from London, as ministers or administrators, with their own ignorances and preconceptions, is individualistic, but undoubtedly an important contribution to historical understanding.'

'If you want to find out what has been going on, and why, over the past 25 years in Northern Ireland, the last person to ask would be a politician. A civil servant would come nearest to the truth, especially one as intelligent, broad-minded and unconventional as Maurice Hayes, whose autobiography deserves to go down as a model of its kind ... Those looking for insider gossip and humour, as well as insight, will find plenty to relish.'

'astute and sometimes acerbic in pithy anecdotes on a number of public personalities'

pb; 234 x 156 mm; 336 pp; £12.99
0-85640-548-5

ORDERING BLACKSTAFF BOOKS

All Blackstaff Press books are available through bookshops.
In the case of difficulty, however, orders can be made
directly to Gill & Macmillan UK Distribution, Blackstaff's
distributor. Indicate clearly the title and number of copies
required and send order with your name and address to:

CASH SALES

Gill & Macmillan UK Distribution
13–14 Goldenbridge Industrial Estate
Inchicore
Dublin 8

Please enclose a remittance to the value of the cover price
plus: £2.50 for the first book plus 50p per copy for each
additional book ordered to cover postage and packing.
Payment should be made in sterling by UK personal cheque,
sterling draft or international money order, made payable to
Gill & Macmillan UK Distribution; or by Access or Visa.

Please debit my Access* Visa* account
*Cross out which is inapplicable

My card number is (13 or 16 digits)

Signature

Expiry date

Name on card

Address

Applicable only in the UK and Republic of Ireland

Full catalogue available on request from
The Blackstaff Press Limited
3 Galway Park, Dundonald, Belfast BT16 0AN
Northern Ireland
Tel. 01232 487161; Fax 01232 489552